MUSIC AND THE MODERN CONDITION: INVESTIGATING THE BOUNDARIES

Two crucial moments in the formation and disintegration of musical modernity and the musical canon occurred at the turn of the seventeenth and the first half of the twentieth century. Dr Ljubica Ilic provides a fresh and close look at these moments, exploring the ways musical compositions shift to and away from ideological structures identified with modernity. The focus is on European art music whose grand narrative, defined by tonality and teleological development, begins in the seventeenth century and ends with twentieth-century modernisms. This particular musical "language game" coincides with historical changes in the phenomenological understanding of space and selfhood. A key concept of the book concerns musical compositions that remain without proper conclusions: if the wholesome (musical) work is a manifestation of wholesome subjectivity, the pieces Ilic explores deny it, reflecting conflict of the individual with previous beliefs, with contexts, and even within the self as the basic modern condition. The musical work is, in this case, still bounded and well-defined, but fractured by the incapability or refusal to satisfactorily conclude: the implicit cut forced upon it changes the expected musical flow or – speaking in spatial terms – it influences the musical form. By using the metaphor of space, Ilic explores: how the existence of a separate self as a primary feature of Western modernity becomes negotiated through awareness of the subject's own independence and individuality; innerness as something entirely separate from its surroundings; and the collective space of social interaction. Seeing musical storytelling as a metaphoric representation of selfhood, and modernity as a historical continuum, Ilic examines the boundaries and relationships between the musical work, the subject, and modern European history.

To Susan

Music and the Modern Condition: Investigating the Boundaries

LJUBICA ILIC

ASHGATE

Published by
Ashgate Publishing Limited
Wey Court East
Union Road
Farnham
Surrey, GU9 7PT
England

Ashgate Publishing Company
Suite 420
101 Cherry Street
Burlington
VT 05401-4405
USA

www.ashgate.com

British Library Cataloguing in Publication Data
Ilic, Ljubica.
  Music and the modern condition : investigating the boundaries.
  1. Music – Psychological aspects. 2. Music – Social aspects.
  I. Title
  781.1'1–dc22

Library of Congress Cataloging-in-Publication Data
Ilic, Ljubica.
  Music and the modern condition : investigating the boundaries / Ljubica Ilic.
    p. cm.
  Includes bibliographical references and index.
  ISBN 978-1-4094-0761-4 (hardcover : alk. paper) — ISBN 978-1-4094-1824-5
  (ebook) 1. Modernism (Music) 2. Music—20th century—History and criticism.
  3. Music—17th century—History and criticism. 4. Music—Social aspects—History.
  I. Title.
  ML193.I55 2010
  780.9'03–dc22

                                                                    2010021641

ISBN 9781409407614 (hbk)
ISBN 9781409418245 (ebk)

Bach musicological font developed by © Yo Tomita.

Mixed Sources
Product group from well-managed forests and other controlled sources
www.fsc.org Cert no. SA-COC-1565
© 1996 Forest Stewardship Council
FSC

Printed and bound in Great Britain by
MPG Books Group, UK

Contents

Introduction
The Limits of the Work,
the Limits of the World

In the early 1960s Umberto Eco elaborated his new theory of the art work. Theoretically rooted in semiotics Eco concludes that in twentieth-century literature "an ordered world based on universally acknowledged laws is being replaced by a world based on ambiguity, both in the negative sense that directional centers are missing and in a positive sense, because values and dogma are constantly being placed in question."[1] In order to describe the literary manifestations of this ambiguous world Eco proposes the new aesthetic category of the "open work" or "*opera aperta*." Interestingly, he finds the most relevant examples of this category not in literature but in twentieth-century music. By looking at the experiments of Pierre Boulez, Karlheinz Stockhausen, Luciano Berio and Henry Pousseur, he defines the open work in opposition to a classical composition that "posits an assemblage of sound units which the composer arranged in a closed, well-defined manner before presenting it to the listener."[2] Noticeably, Eco does not explore experimental practices such as those of John Cage that somehow question the relevance of subjectivity or that, in a Barthean sense, proclaim the death of the author. He is primarily interested in the status of the work of art as a product of the author, seeing the crisis of the work of art as a metaphor for the crisis of the subject's world. Tzvetan Todorov makes use of similar imagery as he explains the way we perceive literature:

> A certain fetishism of the book survives in our own day and age: the literary work
> is transformed both into a precious and motionless object and into a symbol of
> plentitude, and the act of cutting it becomes an equivalent of castration … Only
> an identification of the book with its author explains our horror of cuts.[3]

---

[1]   In the United States, Eco's essay "Poetics of the Open Work" was published independently (Umberto Eco, "The Poetics of the Open Work," trans. Bruce Merry, *Twentieth Century Studies*, no.12, 1974), as well as the part of the collection of his essays: Umberto Eco, *The Open Work*, trans. Anna Cancogni, (Cambridge, MA: Harvard University Press, 1989), pp. 1–24. Throughout this study I will refer to the second source.

[2]   Eco, pp. 2–3.

[3]   Tzvetan Todorov, *The Fantastic: A Structural Approach To a Literary Genre*, trans. Richard Howard (New York: Cornell University Press, 1975), p. 42.

Very similarly Schoenberg defines this problem in music: "it became clear to me that work of art is like every complete organism. It is so homogenous in composition that in every little detail it reveals its truest, inmost essence. When one cuts into any part of the human body, the same thing always comes out – blood."[4]

In following Todorov's and Schoenberg's arguments, the wholesome (musical) work could be understood as a manifestation of (modern) subjectivity, while occurrences of metaphoric "cuts" perform violence on the work's (and thus the subject's) status. Accordingly, when a musical composition remains without a proper conclusion, the implicit cut forced upon it changes the expected musical flow or – speaking in spatial terms – it influences the musical form, thus communicating, as we will see, certain meanings in relation to the subjectivity it expresses.

In the following chapters, I will demonstrate how this analogy between the whole of the work and the whole of the self determines the state of modernity in music. Furthermore, I will explain how this became a burning question in the key moments of the modern condition: its beginning and its decay. By investigating musical storytelling as a metaphoric representation of selfhood and modernity as a historical continuum, I will, if only partly, explore the boundaries and relationships between the musical work, the subject, and modern European history.

Conditio Moderna: **Correspondences and Boundaries**

Manfred Frank's defense of the achievements of modernity directly influenced my use of the term "modern condition:" if there is a definable state of culture and knowledge in postmodern age as Jean-François Lyotard coinage of the "postmodern condition" implies, then there must be the "modern condition" that describes the state of modernity."[5] The discussion on the similarities and differences between modernity and postmodernity, however, is not at the heart of my project; rather, the term "modern condition" conveniently brings together under one expression a set of social and cultural particularities of the historical period of Western modernity. And although I am among those who see more similarities than differences between the two states, there is one certain distinction between them: if the postmodern condition involves plurality and decentralization of narratives in every sense (geography, gender, class, artistic language, and so on), the modern one implies quite the opposite – grand narratives that have a centralizing effect on the structure of society and culture. In relation to music, this implies a focus on European art music whose grand narrative, defined by tonality and teleological development, begins in the seventeenth-century and ends (if only

---

4   Arnold Schoenberg, *Style and Idea*, ed. Leonard Stein, trans. Leo Black (Berkeley, Los Angeles: University of California Press, 1975), p. 144.

5   Frank rightfully goes back to discussing modernity in order to reflect on the attacks of poststructuralists against it. See Manfred Frank, *Conditio Moderna: Essays, Reden, Programm* (Leipzig: Reclam Verlag, 1993).

as a grand narrative) with twentieth-century modernisms. This particular musical "language game" (to refer to both Wittgenstein and Lyotard), is closely interwoven with several other issues of interest that define (musical) modernity; it relates to the problem of both historical and aesthetic boundaries – those of the period of musical modernity and those of musical work; it communicates, through a set of specific musical codes, conflict and crisis as dominant modes of modern culture; it coincides with historical changes in the phenomenological understanding of space and selfhood. Of course, the term "modern condition" implies much more as I will probably suggest from time to time; my focus, however, is on the points delineated above.

My interest in the historical boundaries of modernity occurs, however, maybe somewhat surprisingly, from dealing with standard musical repertoire. While exploring numerous questions related to modern cultural identity expressed in music – questions of representation, self-representation, innerness, and ethics, among others – I realized that I need to examine the shifts to and from the "traditional" "classical" musical vocabulary that we today take for granted: I have to take a closer look into the turn of the seventeenth century and the first half of the twentieth century as the two key moments in the formation and disintegration of musical modernity and the musical canon, exploring the ways musical compositions reflect, and shift to and from, modernity. This is not an easy task. Certain historical questions pertaining to the relationships between modernity and music have not yet been significantly explored. Musicologists usually discuss the music of early modernity, twentieth-century modernism, and finally postmodernism, but they rarely historically explain the relationships between these interconnected phenomena.[6] Taking the first step in this kind of discussion requires tracing the beginnings of ideas that actually culminated in the twentieth-century European avant-garde and American experimentalism. As I will demonstrate, both early modern and late modern crises came about as the results of dissatisfactions with canonical artistic languages. The reasons for the occurrence of both spring from the same well: from the re-questioning of established ideas of Western culture that manifests itself through the crisis in the existing means of expression. In other words, if early modern composers are experimenting and conquering the unknown territory by defining what should constitute the musical piece in order to legitimize it, their late modern counterparts are realizing the crisis of this centuries-old

---

[6]   Recently, however, similar questions have begun to appear in musicological studies. For instance, Daniel Chua eloquently explains the ideological context of developing modernity in order to examine the historical and cultural roots of the category of absolute music. See Daniel K.L. Chua, *Absolute Music and the Construction of Meaning* (Cambridge: Cambridge University Press, 1999). Michael Steinberg, on the other hand, relates the origins of the concept of modern subjectivity to its occurrence of the Enlightenment, juxtaposing it strongly to Baroque culture. See Michael P. Steinberg, *Listening to Reason: Culture, Subjectivity, and Nineteenth-Century Music* (Princeton, NJ: Princeton University Press, 2004).

legitimization; Eco's "ordered world based on universally acknowledged laws" – the laws of tonal and teleological development in the case of music – is here first established and then abolished.

There is a striking similarity, for instance, between the instructions Girolamo Frescobaldi gives in the preface for his *Toccate e partite d'intavolatura* and some post-1945 pieces. Frescobaldi advises:

> In the Toccatas I have attempted to offer not only a variety of passagework and expressive ornaments but also to make the various sections such that can be played independently, so that the performer may stop whenever he wishes and not have to play the entire toccata.[7]

Indeed, the structure of Frescobaldi's toccatas is so sectional that changing the order of sections would not hurt the performance. Yet no matter how much this negation of teleological development resembles some contemporary procedures, one cannot merely relate early modern musical experiments to the avant-garde cases of structural arbitrariness in Boulez's *Third sonata* or Stockhausen's *Klavierstücke*. There is no simple analogy between the works that celebrate musical rhetoric and the ones that specifically go against the "traditional" kind of musical representation. But it is possible to explain how they both relate to what Eco calls "an assemblage of sound units which the composer arranged in closed, well-defined manner before presenting it to the listener."

For both Frescobaldi and Boulez deny the presumption that a musical piece needs to develop from the beginning until the end. Here, the work is not a musical metaphor of history, but rather is a structure that encounters non-musical factors (in Frescobaldi – possible dependence on the sections of the church ritual; in Boulez/ Stockhausen – commentary on the very institution of modern musical work). It follows that in the moments of both the formation and disintegration of modernity (musical) creation is understood differently than in the traditional canon. If these differences sometimes resemble each other, this is so because they are negotiated in the continuum of the same culture. In other words, any discussion "around" the phenomenon of modernity requires a good deal of balancing, without simplifying yet again conventionally oversimplified attempts at unifying the history of the European musical canon. The dangers that can emerge from trying to find common threads in certain trends and systematizing them in a complex net of artistic occurrences are numerous: most likely – the danger of falling into a trap of a mere analogism. On the other hand, every exploration of the ways cultures develop or "think" requires some kind of synthetic approach that enables understanding of why things happen one way instead of another. From this perspective, although dangerous, generalizations are necessary.

---

[7]   Carol MacClintock (ed.), *Readings in the History of Music in Performance* (Bloomington and London: Indiana University Press, 1979), p. 133.

The inspiration for my study comes from the work of authors who, with great depth and insight, dare to make these kinds of generalizations. What reinforced my understanding of similar correspondences between the key moments in the development of modernity, for example, particularly its rise and final crisis, are studies from various humanistic disciplines, beginning with Umberto Eco's theory of *opera aperta*. In explaining the open work, Eco only indicates certain similarities between the early and late modern. In his words:

> If Baroque spirituality is to be seen as the first clear manifestation of modern culture and sensitivity, it is because here, for the first time, man opts out of the canon of authorized responses and finds that he is faced (both in art and in science) by a world in a fluid state which requires corresponding creativity on his part[8]

But many other theorists throughout the twentieth century have eloquently elaborated on this correspondence. The Hungarian-born British art historian Arnold Hauser dedicates a detailed study to the concept of mannerism and its recurrence, especially in the twentieth century.[9] Belgian journalist and writer Gustav René Hocke works on mannerism in both art and literature, constantly referring to twentieth-century art.[10] French essayist and novelist Guy Scarpetta bases his book *The Artifice* on the analogy between the Baroque and twentieth-century art. This is how Scarpetta describes his imaginary transhistorical museum:

> Je rêve de ceci: une exposition où l'on pourrait voir *en même temps* les grandes sculptures du Bernin et les mousquetaires de Picasso. Il est étrange, n'est-ce pas, que personne n'y ait jamais pensé. Faute de mieux, vous pouvez toujours regarder ces mousquetaires en écoutant les *Chants guerriers et amoureux* de Monteverdi.[11]

---

[8]   Eco, p. 7.

[9]   Arnold Hauser, *Mannerism: The Crisis of the Renaissance and the Origin of Modern Art*, trans. Eric Mosbacher (Cambridge: Harvard University Press, 1986).

[10]   Gustav René Hocke, *Die Welt als Labyrinth: Manier und Manie in der Europäischen Kunst* (Hamburg: Rowohlt, 1957).

[11]   Guy Scarpetta, *L'Artifice* (Paris: B. Grasset, 1988), p. 91. In 1934, an exhibition held at the Parisian Museé de l'Orangerie paid tribute to seventeenth-century French artists. Seventy years later, Scarpetta's wish was partially fulfilled by the exhibition "The Painters of Reality" held at the same museum from November 2006 until March 2007 when the same works were complemented by twentieth century paintings that in a similar manner represent everyday life. Another exhibition, held in Roman gallery Borghese between December 2009 and January 2010, places together works by Caravaggio and the Irish twentieth-century painter Frances Bacon.

[I dream of this: an exposition where one could see *at the same time* the grand sculptures of Bernini and Picasso's *Musketeers*. Isn't it strange that no one ever thought of that? For the lack of better, you can always look at the *Musketeers* and listen to Monteverdi's *Songs of War and Peace*.]

And the path that I follow in this book is very close to Hauser's, Hocke's, and Scarpetta's: I put next to each other works by seventeenth-century and twentieth-century composers, trying to discover what is it about their music that awakens the sense that they are somehow similar. What is it in Marini and Monteverdi that resounds in Stockhausen and Berio, what is it in Grandi that we hear again in Schoenberg, and what is it about Stradella that resembles Weill?

Sound, Self and Space: *Wonder at the Long Unbroken Breath Which Pervades the Cosmos*

As some theorists have noticed, the most rigorous studies avoid the term "modernity" "out of semantic decency:" such is the inconsistency in its definitions and chronological demarcations.[12] Indeed, numerous factors influence the emergence of modernity in Western culture: the development of cities, the rise of literacy and "printing culture," the discovery of the new sea routes, the birth of Protestantism, the emergence of empirical science, the rule of reason, the revolutions and changes in class structure, and the development of large-scale capitalism, to name the most common ones. And every one of these factors plays a significant role in explaining the mentality shift from the premodern to modern. The focus of my study, however, is quite specific: I understand modernity as a period in European history from the late sixteenth to the mid-twentieth century, the beginning of which is defined not only by a gradual disintegration of the religious worldview, as it is often claimed, but more importantly, by growing awareness of individual agency in a rapidly changing world. Speaking in stylistic terms, modernity begins with mannerism and the Baroque while its definitive crises arrive with twentieth-century modernism and the avant-garde, when the issues of individuation and personal conflict reach their peak. Throughout this study, I will often use the adjective "early modern" to refer to the period of mannerism and the Baroque, and "late modern" when discussing twentieth-century modernist movements.

Needless to say, it is impossible to give one definition of Renaissance, Baroque or mannerism – the style labels relevant in discussions on early modernity. One faces numerous problems in trying to choose one consistent definition, and because of that my choice is to refer to style discussions only as one source of explanations and interpretations of the art that interests me. For instance, the term "Baroque"

---

[12]   Adrian Marino, *Moderno, modernizam, modernost* (Beograd: Narodna knjiga, 1997), p. 37.

has sometimes been dismissed as a "mostly meaningless period label" because it can become such if we try to include all its possible uses in art history.[13] It is always possible to define it along conventional lines, but there are many other more productive definitions in use; for example, Fernand Braudel claims that the Baroque designates the culture of the Christian Mediterranean that drew its strength from both Roman and Spanish Empires. We cannot, however, limit the Baroque to the art of the Mediterranean area (though that would be extremely convenient in the context of my interest), because significant intellectual and artistic exchange between Southern and Northern Europe cannot be ignored; it is enough only to recall the influence of Italians on Pieter Paul Rubens's paintings and Heinrich Schütz's music, not to mention the great secular art production of what art historians call the Northern Baroque. Lorenzo Bianconi in his study on seventeenth-century music also refuses to use this term claiming that "the 'shape of time' ... has little of the smoothness, consistency and uniformity which the use of such historiographical and stylistic categories as 'baroque' might apply."[14]

In his definition of the "Baroque attitude," however, in only a couple of sentences, Erwin Panofsky manages to embrace the key differences between the High Renaissance, mannerism, and the Baroque: three styles that defined early modernity and that often coexisted:

> The Baroque attitude can be defined as being based on an objective conflict between agonistic forces, which, however, merge into a subjective feeling of freedom and even pleasure: the paradise of the High Renaissance regained after the struggles and tensions of the manneristic period, though still haunted (and enlivened) by the intense consciousness of an underlying dualism.

The fact that these tendencies showed up with less regularity than might be convenient for a consistent theory of style periods does not diminish Panofsky's ability to capture the main traits of particular artistic trends in only a couple of words. It is this brilliance in observation of style theorists that captures my attention and enlivens my own discussion of music.[15]

Arnold Hauser's study on mannerism in art has most influenced the formation of my discussion on modernity. His theory of styles is primarily the history of ideas, in which he, in terms of stylistic analysis, manages to explain the relevant cultural meanings of Western art, never neglecting their historicity. In his opinion, the bases of modern identity and the very birth of Western modern culture arises not with the Renaissance, but with the crisis of humanism expressed in conflicting stylistic traits

---

[13]   Susan McClary, "Mediterranean Trade Routes and Music of the Early Seventeenth Century," *Inter-American Music Review* 17, no. 1–2 (Winter 2007), p. 141.

[14]   See Lorenzo Bianconi, *Music in the Seventeenth Century*, trans. David Bryant (Cambridge: Cambridge University Press, 1982), ix.

[15]   See Erwin Panofsky, "What is Baroque?" *Three Essays on Style*, ed. Irving Lavin (Cambridge, MA: The MIT Press, 1997), p. 45.

of mannerism. The key word for mannerist art, and thus for modernity, is *conflict* precipitated by very specific socio-economic and cultural changes – the conflict of the individual with his previous beliefs, with his surroundings, and even within the self. All these changes created a new awareness of being in the world. In Hauser's words: " ... mannerism was a totally new and unprecedented phenomenon, the first sophisticated deliberately adopted, artistic style of the western world, the first in which one has the feeling of conscious choice rather than of necessity, of driving rather then being driven, of the spontaneous impulse being subjected to control."[16] Hauser's study confirms my belief that modernity arose out of the new born awareness that the inevitable change – good or bad: war, migration, death, disease, decentralization – guides human existence. José Antonio Maravall finds the same conflicting awareness of change in the Baroque: "Mobility, change, inconstancy: all things are mobile and transitory; everything escapes and changes; everything moves, rises or declines, is transferred, gets whirled around. There is no element of which one can be sure that one instant later it will not have changed places or been transformed."[17]

It is, however, rather challenging to apply this "diagnosis" of crisis to the entire continent. For seventeenth-century Europe was a deeply fragmented world: on one side there is a kind of "golden age" in the regions of Spain, France, England, Holland, Sweden, and Denmark, and on the other side, a horrible war disaster in central Europe; the absolutism of France and Prussia is juxtaposed to the constitutionalism of England and Holland while Spain, Italy, and central Europe experience the power of the Counter-Reformation. But if using the term crisis does not seem justified at all times and for all seventeenth-century European regions, it is quite adequate for describing a dominant sentiment at the continent as whole, which experienced altogether only four years of peace.[18]

Indeed, both the 1600s and the 1900s were times of tumultuous social and cultural change; in the 1600s, the constant recurrences of plagues, wars and famines, together with shifts in economic and religious domination, resulted in a society of uncertainty and disorder; in the twentieth century, the enthusiasm

---

[16]   Hauser, p. 28.

[17]   This is how José Antonio Maravall describes this sense of inconsistency in the Spanish seventeenth century. He adds: "Undoubtedly there existed a relationship between the baroque and social crisis. We are faced – not only in Spain, but in all of Europe – with an epoch that, in all spheres of collective life, saw itself dragged along by irrational forces, by appeals to violence, the multiplying of crimes, moral laxity, and hallucinating forms of devotion. All these aspects resulted from the situation of pathos wherein the underlying social crisis was exteriorized and expressed in manifestations of epoch's general mentality." José Antonio Maravall, *Culture of the Baroque: Analysis of a Historical Structure*, trans. by Terry Cochran (Minneapolis: University of Minnesota Press, 1986), p. 53.

[18]   More on this fragmented state of Europe see in Theodore K. Rabb, *The Struggle for Stability in Early Modern Europe* (New York: Oxford University Press, 1975), pp. 7–8.

for industrialization and urbanization on one side, and the regrouping of political powers that led to unseen world conflicts on the other, induced one of the most turbulent periods in European history.[19] In the context of turbulent and unstable times, personal experience also becomes unstable and "fluid." Of course, premodern European history also abounded in economic crises and political turmoil, but those were not reflected in culture and art the same way as in modernity. The key difference, as I will demonstrate, is in the recognition on the part of the modern subject that something could be done against these forces. There is a sense of recognition that change could be also controlled and directed. With the feeling of self-empowerment, however, also comes a sense of responsibility. The question is not only whether a human being could influence his/her surroundings, but also in what measure? What is the limit of human agency? This conflict between desires and restrictions produces modernity's sense of troubled subjectivity and also the angst of what comes after. In my opinion this is the key concept in understanding the modern condition.

Pascal, for example, in his *Pensées* (1670) expresses this fascination with the unknown: "When I consider the short duration of my life, /swallowed up in the eternity before and after/the little space which I fill … /engulfed in infinite immensity of spaces of which/I am ignorant and which know me not, I am frightened/and am being astonished at being here rather than there."[20] Almost a century earlier, Giordano Bruno expressed the same astonishment with the unknown limits of physical existence when arguing *On the Infinite Universe and the Worlds*:

> For the heaven is declared to be a single general space, embracing the infinity of worlds, though we do not deny that there are other infinite 'heavens' using that word in another sense. For just as this earth hath her own heaven (which is her own region), through which she moveth and hath her course, so the same may be said of each of the innumerable other worlds.

---

[19]   Despite the fact that early modern Europe was by any standard a deeply fractured world and that this fracturedness returns to an even greater extent in the first half of the twentieth-century, European regional cultures were always in significant interaction. In both moments, art and culture took on an international character. In a politically fractured and conflicted world, artists recognized the common grounds of Western cultural identity. Giacomo Carissimi (1605–1674) and Alessandro Stradella (1642–1682) worked in Rome; Alessandro Grandi (1575–1630) held employment in Ferrara, Venice and Bergamo, but his music attained a vast popularity throughout the Apennines; Biagio Marini (1594–1663) composed the piece I will discuss while serving at the Wittelsbach court at the Neuburg an di Donau. All of them worked under the direct influence of the Catholic Church and courts that even reached the Protestant works of Heinrich Schütz (1585–1672). And this connecting thread becomes much stronger in the twentieth century. Arnold Schoenberg's (1874–1951), Kurt Weill's (1900–1950), Karlheinz Stockhausen's (1928–2007) and Luciano Berio's (1925–2003) modernist experiments, which I will explore, influenced, at least to some extent, every culture in which Western musical modernity played a significant role.

[20]   John Rupert Martin, *Baroque* (Pelican Books: 1989), pp. 155–196.

Bruno's negation of geocentrism resulted in the human recognition of its own diminished significance, but at the same time it discovered the possibilities of the entire new world of subjective experience that we read in Pascal's poetic reflections.

Art historians who wrote on the Baroque found the same amazement – the sense of infiniteness that Bruno and Pascal describe – in numerous artworks of the time. Definition of the visual whole, related to the perception of space, either real (in architecture and sculpture) or fictive (in painting) significantly changed in comparison to the Renaissance. John Rupert Martin, in his study on the Baroque, dedicates the entire chapter to the exploration of spatial boundaries in artworks of the seventeenth century.[21] He elaborates that in the Baroque, the barrier between the work of art and the real world becomes broken down as if the observer and the observed object coexist in a unified space, in a continuous and unbroken totality that becomes infinite. This interaction between the real space of the spectator and the fictive space of the painting functions as *trompe l'oeil*, quite the opposite from the Renaissance concept of the painting as a "window into space."[22] Heinrich Wölfflin also discusses space as one of the most important themes of Baroque art. He writes about undefined boundaries of Baroque artworks and the content, which, as if moving, seems "to want to jump out" from the boundaries of a picture frame.[23] It is enough to mention Pietro da Cortona's illusionist ceiling in Roman palazzo Barberini, in which the space of the represented skies and the space of the observer become one, or Bernini's statue of David who, as if moving, looks fiercely into the space in front of him while the spectator imagines what is not represented, but nevertheless present: the enemy (Goliath) or any other presence to which David's gaze is addressed. Arnold Hauser finds in that unlimitedness of space, as well as many other elements, what he calls "anti-classical tendencies," which arise during mannerism and that laid foundations for early modernity. He claims that:

> the most striking feature of mannerist anticlassicism, however, was its abandonment of *the fiction that a work of art is an organic, indivisible, and invulnerable whole, made all of a piece* ... A non-classical work always seems like *an open, uncompleted system*, no matter whether the incompleteness is attributable to an unmastered abundance of experience or to an intellectual conception the breath and depth of which have burst the classical bonds. Consciously or unconsciously, non-classical art abandons the fiction that artistic creation constitutes a self-contained world with impossible boundaries, a precinct which, once having been entered, cannot be left again.[24]

---

[21]   Ibid.

[22]   Ibid., pp. 155–157.

[23]   Heinrich Wölfflin, *Renaissance and Baroque*, trans. Katharine Simon (Ithaca, NY: Cornell University Press, 1966).

[24]   The italic emphasis is mine. See Hauser, pp. 24–25.

Applying such non-musical discussions to music is quite difficult and challenging. Music historians adopted style labels like the Baroque with a rather pragmatic purpose: it made music history surveys easier to organize.[25] The characteristics of musical styles were understood quite independently from those of the other arts, and successful connections and comparisons of music with other arts were rarely made. Although music historians borrowed style categories from the history of fine arts, they appropriated and adjusted them as if they were inherent to music history. This project becomes a logical tendency in the context of an emerging music autonomy that both Lydia Goehr and Daniel Chua discuss and situate around the turn of the eighteenth century.[26]

I believe that the concept of musical style came into use in a similar manner as musical autonomy, inspired by the same desire to validate the productiveness of music, and in addition by a desire to categorize music history for easier comprehension. But, for the sake of the promotion of music autonomy, the traces of the origins of both concepts subsequently got lost. This, in my opinion, has had a damaging influence on thinking about music.[27] The one useful reason for

---

[25]   Most music histories and music history textbooks are divided up on the basis of style periods: the Oxford History of Music, for instance, or the Norton series are among the popular ones.

[26]   Goehr claims: "As music began to be understood first and foremost as one of the fine arts, it began clearly to articulate its need for enduring products – artifacts comparable to other works of fine art. Hence the emergence of a work-concept in the field of music in the mid- to late- eighteenth century. As the work-concept formed, emphasis began to be but on those very same conditions associated with the other fine arts, conditions previously underemphasized, or overridden by others, in the history of music. In this respect, then, the origins of the concept of a work of music are to be found less in the history of music before the 1750s than in the history of the productive arts." Lydia Goehr, *The Imaginary Museum of Musical Works: An Essay in the Philosophy of Music* (Oxford: Oxford University Press, 1994), p. 152. Looking into historically defined moments of the emergence and disintegration of modernity as points in Western culture between which artistic work existed as autonomous activity, independent and "protected" from extra-aesthetical meanings does not necessarily call for replicating this ideological framework: discussing musical pieces in order to place them in "the imaginary museum of musical works" does not seem as necessary today. As Goehr explains, this is a concept born out from romantic ideology – culturally and historically specific (governed by the standards of fine arts) and, more importantly, quite restrictive when applied to music created in other contexts.

[27]   In this context, "the musical work" signifies any product of musical creativity: *musics* produced for court and church as well as music deliberately composed for concert performance or contemplation as an autonomous activity for its own sake. From this perspective, any human activity such as music-making can be understood as a *work* of human imagination and a product of the need for a meaningful expression. This kind of definition does not diminish the importance of aesthetics or historiography, but it gives an advantage to cultural perspective. It is not only music's aesthetic qualities that matter but also the social and cultural characteristics of the historical moment in question. The problem of the artistic whole transcends the questions of artistic autonomies that Eco's and

discussing music as a style would be its contextualization in relation to the other arts and general cultural trends. However, the logic of music history did not "fit in" well chronologically or aesthetically with other arts. Thus, music history has a significantly independent theory of styles that to a great extent neglects the general cultural and historical contexts from which it originated.[28]

Moreover, style labels have persisted in part because they enable the discussing of music without any obligation to decipher meanings that reach beyond its autonomous existence. Rare are studies of style in music like the astonishing study of mannerism by Maria Rika Maniates, who makes brilliant connections between music and the general historical and cultural context of the time.[29] Maniates has not had sufficient influence, though, on thinking about early modern music. Aesthetic autonomy is so influential in thinking about musical modernity that cross-disciplinary approaches have been underappreciated. Even Adorno did not recognize the effects of seventeenth-century music, claiming that the largely undeveloped, primitive, rudimentary, and undifferentiated music of the thorough-bass period really has nothing in common with the "late" painting style of mannerism apart from the fact that they all existed at the same time.[30]

Susan McClary, however, claims that the emergence of basso continuo and the first "realistic" musical representations of subjectivity in genres like opera, concerto, and sonata denote the inauguration of the tonal era that, in one way or another, persists until today.[31] Although far from sharing Adorno's opinion, I do admit that the phenomenological differences between the various arts complicate any obvious, simple analogy. But what I want to show is that this analogy, although not simple, is possible and helpful. Studies like McClary's, which attribute meaning to early modern music, create intellectual paths that make this analogy easier to conduct.

It may seem strange, however, not to include Romantic artworks in this discussion of the deterioration of tradition. There are many instances in music from late Beethoven through Mahler, for example, that I could use in order to do so. But in the history of musical forms, there is a continuous line of development from the late Baroque, when the main codes of canonic classical music were established, to late Romanticism, when these familiar codes disintegrated. I

Todorov's ideas necessarily evoke. The history of music, like art history, reveals several crises concerning the notion of a musical creation as a logical (rational, natural) whole, not necessarily bounded by the author/work concept.

[28]   In music, the most consistent, elaborated and justified is the use of the term "classical style." Yet its definition is entirely derived from musical characteristics.

[29]   Maria Rika Maniates, *Mannerism in Italian Music and Culture, 1530–1630* (Chapel Hill: The University of North Carolina Press, 1979).

[30]   Theodor W. Adorno, *Sound Figures*, trans. Rodney Livingston (Stanford, CA: Stanford University Press, 1999), p. 109.

[31]   Susan McClary, *Modal Subjectivities: Self-Fashioning in the Italian Madrigal* (Berkeley: University of California Press, 2004), pp. 4–5.

avoid discussing the Romantic reaction against established order because the Romantics understood the inwardness they expressed as something unchangeable, true and unique. In Romanticism, the fragmentation of musical structure mirrors a fractured subjectivity. Charles Rosen emphasizes, however, that the fragment, "imperfect and yet complete" in Romanticism, becomes a virtue. He refers to Friedrich Schlegel's writings on fragments in which he claims that "a fragment should be like a little work of art, complete in itself and separated from the rest of the universe like a hedgehog." The work, thus, is perfect in its imperfection. In order to be perceived as true, it has to be fractured. This belief in incompleteness as a state of being cannot be farther removed from the early and late modern experimentations that "want" to resist any possible dogma. In relation to musical structure: in order to appear as true, and thus organically developed, Romantic fissure occurs from inside to outside; it explodes, while early and late modern versions of incompleteness result from conscious deliberation; they are rhetorical, they ask questions.[32] Charles Rosen rightly refers to Benjamin's conclusions on theatrical procedures in order to clarify this significant difference: "in the Baroque the deliberate destructions of stage illusion served to show that life is an illusion like a play; in the Romantic period they attempt to give a new status to the work, to persuade us that art is real life."[33]

Indeed, Baroque sensibility is based on high awareness of artifice and convention, and in this sense it resembles more closely the twentieth-century breakaway from the canon. The similarity between the early and late versions of musical modernity lies in their power to reconstitute the world, not only to stretch its limits, but to build it all over again. The similarity between the two also lies in their respective critiques of the Renaissance and Enlightenment projects while Romanticism often thrives on the elevation of ideas to the point of religious fervor. But my intention is not, as it is fairly popular in contemporary criticism under the influence of critical theory and post-structuralism, to negate the project of the Enlightenment. My interest in the limits of the subject (world, work) is foremost historical. It is guided by the fascination with the mentality shifts in Western history in which the unpredictable play of cultural codes reveals unexpected and exciting connections.

And these mentality shifts are most transparent in the ways cultures understand concepts such as space. Moreover, to go back to my previous discussion, I believe that the essence of modern experience is in the exploration of the boundaries of real and metaphorical spaces, the exploration that becomes especially relevant in the moments when modernity arises and deteriorates. After all, the notion of space as something separate from the subject is possible only with the modern understanding of the world: the premodern individual – as I will demonstrate on the example of

---

[32] For further discussion on the romantic fragment, see Charles Rosen, "Fragments," *The Romantic Generation* (Cambridge, Massachusetts: Harvard University Press, 1995), pp. 41–112.

[33] Ibid., p. 78.

court entertainments in the first chapter – would hardly understand space as an autonomous category, or create boundaries between the self (microcosm) and the rest of the world (macrocosm). The clear distinction between the categories of time and space and their use as "empty," abstract concepts is the key factor for the dynamism of modernity: in premodern understanding of the world, "when" is always related to "where," usually determined by events guided by natural cycles.[34] In the Middle Ages, there is no even an adequate word to signify the term space: *spatium* meant distance while *locus* determined the place inhabited by the body.[35] Space, as an abstraction, was not recognized. Spatial autonomy, first physical and then metaphorical (social, cultural, personal, and so on) becomes possible only when the sense of self is such – autonomous, individualistic – that it sees everything else in relation to its own centricity.[36]

In the first chapter, I discuss phenomenological characteristics of spatial relations in the transition from premodern to modern music performance. I show how an understanding of physical space changes fundamentally the nature of music making. Secondly, by using the metaphor of space I explore how the existence of a separate self as the primary feature of Western modernity becomes negotiated through awareness of: (1) the subject's own independence and individuality ("Mirrors and Echoes: Beyond the Confines of the Theatrical Space"); (2) innerness as something entirely separate from its surroundings, a space of its own ("The Unutterable Silence: *O Word Thou Word that I Lack*"); (3) the collective space of social interaction ("The Terror of Desire: Arbitrary Outcomes or the *Dei ex Machinis*"). First, I observe compositions that experiment with the notion of sound in the physical space of the theater stage, as in seventeenth-century echo pieces and twentieth-century electronic music. I discuss pieces by Jacopo Peri, Claudio Monteverdi, Biagio Marini, Heinrich Schütz, Luciano Berio, and Karlheinz Stockhausen. My further focus is on the issues of the inner space of the subject and its theatrical display. I look at compositions that document the emergence and disintegration of modern subjectivity defined by conscious self-reflection. Here I deal with the relationship between secularization and modernity. In spite of popular belief, these compositions suggest that early modernity was partially formed on religious fervor. In the compositions by Alessandro Grandi, Benedetto Ferrari, Heinrich Schütz, Giacomo Carissimi, and Arnold Schoenberg in which formal conclusions become suddenly interrupted or "collapsed" I discuss the inner self that becomes overwhelmed with religious ecstasy. The final focus is

[34]   Anthony Giddens, *The Consequences of Modernity* (Stanford: Stanford University Press, 1990), pp. 17–21.

[35]   See an excellent discussion on medieval culture: Aron Gurevich. *Categories of Medieval Culture*, trans. G.L. Campbell (London, Boston: Routledge & Kegan Paul, 1985).

[36]   The discovery of geographically remote territories and their symbolic representation influenced the creation of distinction between the categories of place and their spatial abstraction (maps).

on the notion of the musical work as an independent space governed by seemingly autonomous laws of musical language; at the center of my attention is the dramatic strategy of *Deus Ex Machina* used by seventeenth-century composers Alessandro Stradella and Claudio Monteverdi, and twentieth-century composer Kurt Weill. I look at the meanings of dramatically illogical resolutions of the works of musical theater in order to explain their ethical implications.

Upon the first glance, it may seem that these are three different definitions of selfhood: phenomenological, psychological, and cultural. But I don't believe that is the case. My metaphorical use of space does not originate from this kind of separation. For I believe that all these spaces are deeply connected and intertwined. In other words, I do not want to operate rhetorically between constant binarisms of interiority and exteriority, the individual and the collective, psychology and culture. I believe that these conventionally opposed forces always work simultaneously. And in my discussion, I try to bring them together and show how they are inseparable.

Finally, I will refer to a customary use of the metaphor of space to point out changes in musical meanings – the common way of representing music as an abstract form; music, however, is a temporal medium, and to conclude a musical piece usually means to go back to its introductory mode (defined most often by pitch and tonality, but also by affect, dynamics, and other musical characteristics) as the most common point of reference. In the pieces that draw my attention, however, composers perform a deliberate obstruction of this "natural" order of things by getting delighted by their own creativity, expressing emotional exhaustion, "estranging" the familiar starting point, posing a question, renouncing catharsis, denying the existence of satisfied subjectivity, or communicating the impossibility of harmonious community, among many other things. The key dilemma these pieces pose is how to tell a story, and more importantly, how to end it. As in classical oratory that comprises introduction, development, and conclusion, there is a sense that music should end with some kind of conclusive logic. I attempt to show that this logic has often been called into question, thus metaphorically displaying a sense of human self-empowerment, and its potential to manipulate the world. If self-agency always shows both sides of its face, enthusiasm as well as angst, it is the sense of anxiety that persistently creates the impossibility of conclusion.[37]

---

[37]   What is this "self" to which I refer? Is it the composer's, performer's, or interpreter's perspective that I take into account? My position involves the totality of perspectives that I can imagine. When discussing music, I try to include all possible experiences of it: I try to imagine the historical situation, I try to read the text as it is preserved, I listen to all existing performances, I imagine the new ones. I don't want to claim that I know the composer's intentions or that I somehow understand how audiences exactly felt when listening to it. But I believe that every writing about the past involves the work of the imagination. No matter how much I desire a history that is objective, I do not believe in that possibility. Every writing of history is also its rewriting. In any case, my wish would be to contribute

Several times in this discussion I mentioned the issue of autonomy – the autonomy of the self, the autonomy of space, the autonomy of music – as the key factor in understanding modernity. This apparently ordered, stable world of clear autonomous categories (even when they seem forced as in the case of musical style) reflects confidence in rationality so typical for the modern condition. When commenting on the enthusiasm about the possibility of the systematic, all-encompassing knowledge contained in Hegel's claim that "truth is the whole," however, Adorno bitterly answers back: "The whole is untrue."[38] Adorno is thinking of social totalitarianism, but his rejection of the totality could be easily transposed to the realm of aesthetic: that is exactly where his interest in Schoenberg's negation of the logic of tonal development comes from. In the final chapter, I will try to make a connection between the notion of the whole and the ethical implications that Adorno's counterstatement evokes. By adding an ethical interpretation to the phenomenological and aesthetical analyses of the first and second chapters I will create a full interpretative circle, trying to clarify why wholeness becomes an ethically unacceptable, and paradoxically, even disturbing category.

There are several intriguing questions to which answers I might, at least partially, contribute to by the end of this study. How might we address the traditional musical canon in the aftermath of (post)modernity and (post)modernism? How should we interpret "classical" musical works in a time of constant requisitioning and redefining art and the artwork (or if they still even exist)? If art can be understood now not only as a fixed text, but also as an action, happening, performance, or experiment produced by one or more persons – author(s), artist(s), producer(s), troupe, collective, and so on – how should we treat what is today seen as the traditional paradigm against which all these "alternative" artistic practices developed in the first place? How might we ask non-musical questions but not exclusively in relation to the works of composers who consciously take up this issue by exploring the limits of the musical discipline, and even broadening the concept of art to the point when it becomes life (for example, John Cage)? What interests me most is how to investigate the traditional, canonical language in a manner that enables insights into meanings that are both cultural and philosophical. And last but not the least: how can we avoid essencializing one culture, history, and identity? In other words, discussing a great master narrative of European "classical" music from the position of a postmodern subject immersed in cultural pluralism and proliferation of language games, without trying to somehow dethrone, deconstruct, or demystify its centralized position is quite challenging. My hope is that there are still many issues that we can take from understanding our modern heritage in order to appreciate it for what it is rather for what we want it to be.

The transnational context of this study, conducted by a Southeastern European (thus encompassing several cultural identities – Middle European, Mediterranean,

---

to the meaningful advance of music that is very often forgotten or superseded. And the self to which I refer includes contemporary perspectives as much as it refers to past ones.

[38]   I owe this observation to Manfred Frank.

and Oriental) educated at a North American university certainly broadens the theoretical perspective. This position is decentralized in more than one way because it deals with the standard repertory as experienced in cultural contexts removed from the geographical center, echoed and mirrored against the presence of other cultural influences; in my case, from the borders where the modern bourgeois culture of the Mitteleuropa and the Oriental (and in many aspects premodern) culture of the Balkans meet; and, more recently, from the perspective of, in many aspects postmodern, Anglo-American experience. Because of this background, I can never understand the heritage of Western modernity as something self-evident. And although I will not specifically discuss its theoretical implications, I believe that this state of dividedness and permanent "otherness" greatly shapes my arguments, constantly reinscribing – whether intentionally or not – a sense of cultural detachment in my discussion.

Chapter 1
Mirrors and Echoes:
Beyond the Confines of Theatrical Space[1]

Perception of the Mirroring Image

The "horror of cuts," by which Todorov describes our habits in regarding literature, is very often consciously manipulated within twentieth-century artistic poetics. In 1935, Max Ernst created an unusual invitation for one of his exhibitions: the text of the invitation appears in the cracks of a photographic collage, representing Ernst's face as if seen in a shattered mirror. The distorted self-imagery of Ernst's portrait, originally taken by Man Ray, reflects a recurrent problem of self-representation in Western art that reached its peak in twentieth-century Dadaism and Surrealism. But the earliest examples of this kind of intricate self-portraiture originate in the sixteenth and seventeenth centuries. Already in 1524, Parmigianino, in his famous self-portrait, revealed his fascination with the optics of the convex mirror and the distorting effect it creates. Even earlier – in 1508 – Leonardo planned to build, among other inventions, a chamber of eight mirrors in which the mirroring object would become visible from every side: when standing in the middle of it, the observer would be overwhelmed with the number of possible viewpoints and with his or her own de-centered gaze. In *The Order of Things*, Foucault showed the ever-changing logic of human perspective by explaining the behind-the-mirror gaze of the beholder in front of Velásquez's *Las Meninas*.[2] The painter himself and all the other protagonists in the painting seem to look at the mirror while the gaze of the spectator comes from somewhere behind it; there is nothing that could logically bridge the space that stands between the imaginary mirror and the potential witness of this scene. In *Las Meninas*, Velásquez puts the observer inside the mirror, in an unreal, infinite space that seems unusually familiar today because of its similarity to the voyeuristic perspective of the camera.

The representation of the self in respect to the surrounding space poses the key question: how are we to understand ourselves in the world? This question may seem applicable to any number of possible historical and cultural contexts,

---

[1]   One part of this discussion was published as "Echo and Narcissus: Labyrinths of the Self in Early Modern Music," in Jessica Goethals, Valerie McGuire and Gaoheng Zhang (eds), *Power and Image in Early Modern Europe* (Cambridge Scholars Publishing, 2008), pp. 43–55, and has been reproduced by permission of Cambridge Scholars Publishing.

[2]   Michel Foucault, *The Order of Things: An Archeology of the Human Sciences*, trans. Rupert Swyer (New York: Random House Inc., 1994), pp. 3–16.

but in the cases of art works that quite literally reflect the artist, it becomes the main preoccupation. There are two aspects of self-reflection that I find especially important in the context of art and culture of modernity: the sense of the self in the surrounding world and the exploration of the powers and limits of personal agency. These two aspects condition each other, but at this point I want to focus on the first one. In the previous examples, for instance, the artists explore self-perception in the context of their environments. Leonardo, Parmigianino, and Velásquez experiment with the possibilities of representation while exploring the physical laws that govern human perceptual experience. Parmigianino's mannerist fascination with the elongated shape of his own hand, the disoriented perspective in Leonardo's chamber of multiple mirrors, and the small unusual details in Velásquez's court scenery (like the royal couple left out of the room but nevertheless represented in the small mirror at the center of the painting, as Foucault points out) – all communicate a desire for expressing reality that is subverted not by imagining the unimaginable, but by intensifying and multiplying the sensory effect of actual realistic representation. Like their late modern counterparts such as Ernst, they indulge in representations that are slightly convoluted and very often enigmatic. It is easy to recognize the negation of realism in the use of fantastic or anti-representational (or anti-naturalistic) imagery. But what does mean to go beyond realistic representation by intensifying it? This kind of representational exaggeration brings about a very specific set of problems in the understanding of the world: the reflection in the mirror can be perfectly clear on one hand, but it can be distorted or cracked, on the other. What is questioned in such works is the legitimacy of the one who represents and describes the reality and him- or herself.

While portraiture has a long tradition of signifying the social power, hierarchical status, and wealth of the subject represented, self-portraiture in a majority of cases testifies to quite opposite motivating forces. Self-portraiture was created for practical yet unpragmatic reasons; its basic purpose was experimentation with physical likeness and the scrutiny of the model – an enterprise usually not supported financially by the patron. In any case, a complex net of motives is at play. Early modern self-portraits figure the artist's physical likeness, interior states, desires, and sometimes the projection of social status. Bernini, for example, loved to represent himself as a powerful figure like Mars, David, or Alexander the Great.[3] Similarly, Rubens created a series of portraits that testify to his social rank. Rembrandt, on the other hand, with his self-portraiture offers both a guide through the evolution of his painting style, and a window into his psychological and emotional changes – a kind of self-indulgence recognizable as early as in self-portraits by Albrecht Dürer.

---

[3]   Otto Dix (1891–1969) in his *Self-portrait as Mars* (1915) refers to Bernini. Dix's expressionist distortion, however, carries a strong disillusionment with the God of war, depicting Dix's inner turmoil upon facing war atrocities. I will discuss this self-awareness and criticism toward society as a byproduct of the Enlightenment in my final chapter.

This interest in self-representation was probably enhanced by the increasing use of mirrors all over Europe. The mirror as we know it today, a plate of flat glass with a sheet of reflecting metal, was invented by sixteenth-century Venetian artisans, whose secret spread out throughout Europe in the seventeenth and eighteenth centuries. This luxurious object became a token of wealth, used in everyday life of rich households, and also for the first steps of empirical science, as a part of the telescope. The mirror becomes a metaphor for the border of reality: a window to the other side of human perception; something evident in many mannerist artworks and throughout the entire history of modernity from Leonardo to surrealists.

Its significance as a metaphor for interiority becomes irreplaceable in psychoanalytical theory. My focus, however, is not on interiority in a psychoanalytical sense. What interests me are the reasons and surrounding circumstances that led to interior changes, the phenomenological and then social and cultural conditions that primarily describe the collective and exteriority. Even when speaking in psychoanalytical terms, I am interested in defining the collective rather than individual unconscious, in discussing culture rather than psychology. In other words, I find intriguing not the projection of interiority as much as the relationship with the surrounding world and the conditions that precede and shape it; not the psychology, but the understanding of selfhood, never completely divided from the notion of power, always primarily focused on the phenomenology of physical existence. In Foucault's words:

> The fact that within the space of a few years a culture sometimes ceases to think as it had been thinking up till then and begins to think other things in a new way – probably begins with an erosion from outside, from that space which is, for thought, on the other side, but in which it had never ceased to think from the very beginning.[4]

My involvement with self-portraiture has the goal of confirming the understanding of artistic occurrences as historical reflections of changes in cultural mentality. To be clearer: the need for self-representation occurred at a certain time in history, for very particular reasons. It is a project that defines Western modernity as the period in which the questions of selfhood dominate among others. As many now concur, modernity is defined by the supremacy of human gaze. In Martin Jay's words, modernity is an ocularcentric culture, a culture that values sight above the other senses.[5] The domination of visual perception, especially after the discovery of perspective, significantly influenced perceptions of space in both the non-performing and performing arts.[6]

---

[4]   Foucault, p. 50.

[5]   Martin Jay, *Downcast Eyes: The Denigration of Vision in Twentieth-Century French Thought* (Berkeley: University of California Press, 1993), p. 3.

[6]   The intensity of our contemporary everyday involvement in visual culture cannot be compared with our relationship to the auditory one. The circulation of images in all aspects

Echo and Narcissus

It is not only that the visual arts engage in concerns of self-representation but that the same is true of music: the works of the modern musical canon reveal understandings of selfhood just as portraiture and other genres of art do. The equivalent of the historical trajectory of European art from Parmigianino to Ernst that I traced earlier has its equivalent in music.

To begin with, the correspondences between visual and aural reflections in Western culture are at least as old as Ovid's story of Narcissus and Echo. According to ancient mythology, the goddess Juno punished the nymph Echo for excessive talkativeness by condemning her to eternal mimicking of the speech of her collocutors. Narcissus, on the other hand, is in ancient sources conventionally presented as a beautiful and vain boy who dies of love for his own reflection. In *Metamorphoses*, Ovid brings the two characters together, using Echo's incapability to foretell Narcissus's own unfortunate destiny. He unites the two characters in their sins of self-love – Narcissus's negligence of others and Echo's overindulgence in words. Sixteenth-century epigram encapsulates this analogy: "Well-deserving are you now punished, Narcissus, most fair youth, as you deserve, and your face now by right captivates you. Echo gave you back the words without reaching her goal, now without reaching your goal you are in search of yourself."[7]

In Ovid's version, Echo is the one among the many enamored of Narcissus. When she has finally collected enough courage to address him, she is, owing to Juno's punishment, only capable of repeating Narcissus's final words. Thus, Ovid

---

of our culture, and especially in media made the Western visual arts far more approachable and understandable to wider audiences than "classical" music. Canonical musical works are fairly well represented at the concert stage and in the recording industry, but never as much as the Western visual arts. The constant reinterpretation of the meanings of Western artworks oftentimes blurs the importance of the images' initial meanings, but simultaneously reempowers their status in eyes of newer and younger audiences. Musical equivalents of the *Mona Lisa* or *The Last Supper* do exist – we need only remind ourselves of the overexposure of Pachelbel's *Canon* in D or Tchaikovsky's *Nutcracker* in the contemporary context – but they cannot compare with the proliferation and power that images have in our time. This is not to say that music does not affect us. On the contrary, think of our daily immersion in music in almost every aspect of our lives. This immersion is evident in the popularity of the portable pleasure of mp3 players, which can store hours of music, at the individual's disposal almost anywhere. It is true, however, that musical experiences are more visceral, less conscious, and thus more difficult to talk about. We do not usually analyze music consciously as we do the images that surround us. That is why, in order to say more about music and its history, to make it more approachable and closer to our cultural, aesthetic, and even ethical experiences, I often refer to visual imagery as something that we intuitively understand better.

[7]   Epigram by Johannes Franciscus Apostolius (16th century) as quoted in Louise Vinge, *The Narcissus Theme in Western European Literature up to the Early 19th Century* (Lund: Skånska Centaltryckeriet, 1967), p. 162.

uses Echo's discursive weakness not only to emphasize Narcissus's power, the ineffability of his beauty, but also to foreshadow Narcissus's final downfall: in a conversation with his potential lover, Narcissus's words only bounce back at him in the same way his reflection will stare back from the brook once he falls in love with his own image. In other words, the relationship between Narcissus and Echo is metaphorically reciprocal to Narcissus's inability to be infatuated with anyone but himself. As Narcissus's Other, Echo is merely his aural reflection; she's an aural metaphor for his visual self-infatuation. Their mutual fate is to lose their original appearances: rejected and ashamed Echo hides in woods and caves; as her love grows, she wastes away until she becomes only a voice; Narcissus fades away of love with his own reflection, transforming himself into a flower.

In *The Metamorphoses*, Narcissus is a sad figure, the victim of a judgment error who gets caught in a moment of illusion. He does not come across as a character who consciously adores his own image, because he becomes aware only rather late in the story that he's actually in love with himself; although properly punished for being vain and refusing the love of all the nymphs (including Echo), he does not show any capability for inner reflection.[8] To quote Julia Kristeva: "*The object of Narcissus is psychic space; it is representation itself, fantasy. But he does not know it, and he dies. If he knew it he would be an intellectual, a creator of speculative fictions, an artist, writer, psychologist, psychoanalyst. He would be Plotinus or Freud.*"[9] After Ovid, however, the myth went through significant transformations and reinterpretations, offering differing lessons depending upon the cultural agenda of the particular narrator. In early modern culture, it took a life of its own, inspired by, yet quite independent of ancient sources. In Renaissance lyrical poems, for instance, it depicted unhappy love, while in emblematic and didactic poetry it became an allegory of vanity. Whatever the interpretation of the myth, however, Echo always ends up alone. Thus she and the actual acoustic phenomenon named after her seemed to offer the perfect metaphor for an early modern subjectivity that recognizes both the possibilities and the limits of its own agency.

---

[8] Even after recognizing his mistake (*"Why, you're me! Now I see. My reflection has deceived me! I'm in love with myself! I light the fire that I feel! What am I going to do? Wait for him to make the first move? Make it myself? How can I make the first move now? What I want, I've got; what I've got, I want. Oh! If only I could leave my body! Here's a new prayer for a lover: 'Go away, my love!'*), Narcissus does not manage to utterly grasp it. (*"Half out of his mind with grief, he looked again at the face in the pool, and his tears, splashing into the water, broke up the reflection: 'Where are you running away to?' he cried when he saw the image disappearing. 'Stay with me, heartless boy...'"*) Ovid, *The Metamorphoses*, trans. and introduction by Michael Simpson (Amherst: University of Massachusetts Press, 2001), p. 55.

[9] Julia Kristeva, "Narcissus: The New Insanity," *Tales of Love*, trans. Leon S. Roudiez (New York: Columbia University Press, 1987), p. 116.

The early modern love of echo rhetoric was influenced by the popularity of mimetic representation in music. Within this framework, the effect of sound reflection was very often used to depict physical space – not only the resounding of mythical meadows where Echo and Narcissus supposedly met, or the spatial settings of other mythical, biblical, and historical stories, but also the actual physical space of the performing venue. The evocation of space through the juxtaposition of multiple sources of sound and an emphasis on the material distance between them is crucial for the effect of echoing. In performances like these, the players or singers who imitate the resounding voice respond from behind the scene or from the opposite side of the performing venue, sonically simulating the acoustics of a pastoral landscape. The musical imitations of natural phenomena like echoing very often developed into complex aural illusions that significantly surpass realistic representation.

The echo appears in various forms and in nearly all early modern musical genres. It plays a prominent role in dramatic settings of madrigals and operas; it becomes incorporated as an extra feature in the spatial games of antiphonal choirs and in the registrar experiments of organ music; it was used to exploit relationships between sound and space in instrumental music composed for acoustically resonant chapels and cathedrals. In choral settings, and especially in madrigals, it functioned as an auditory game; its mimetic nature offered a great deal to composers who wanted to play with possibilities of musical representation. In the *Garden of Eloquence* Henry Peacham explains echoing as a specific form of repetition: "This exornation doth not only serve to the pleasantness of sound, but also to adde a certaine increase in the second member. Of some this figure is called the Rhetoricall Eccho, for that it carrieth the resemblance of a rebounded voice, or iterated sound."[10] The rhetoric of echo could express a wide range of emotions, from lamentation to rhetorical potency. For instance, Orlando di Lasso's famous "Echo song" (*Ola, o che bon echo!*) revels in the simulation of resounding voices: the protagonists in the song recognize the resonance and then play with it just for fun; the brisk and jovial lyrics take part in this joke, and the entire piece delights in the simple effect of echoing. But the earliest use of echo effects in court entertainments brings about an entirely different set of issues: it reflects the mentality change in understanding space and selfhood in the genre of *intermedi*.

Effetti Meravigliosi: Between Affectation and Illusion

Numerous documents testify to the rising popularity of *intermedi* in the second half of the sixteenth century. When writing about this genre, music historians often emphasize the complaints of the contemporary playwright Antonfrancesco

---

[10]   Dietrich Bartel, *Musica Poetica: Musical-Rhetorical Figures in German Baroque Music* (Lincoln and London: University of Nebraska Press, 1997), p. 343.

Grazzini: "Once the *intermedi* were made to serve the comedy, but now comedies are made to serve the *intermedi*," he writes.[11] It seems that surprising stage effects, created by cloud machines and stage traps, made these entr'actes much more appealing to court audiences then the very plays they were interpolated into. Valuable testimonies about the performance of *intermedi* offer a substantial amount of information as to what these performances looked like. Some of them, for example, suggest that the space surrounding the stage of *intermedi* was not concealed from viewers' eyes. From one of the descriptions of the wedding of Francesco de' Medici and Joanna of Austria in 1565, we learn that in *intermedi* organized for that occasion, dealing with Appulius' fable of Cupid and Psyche, and performed in between the acts of Francesco d'Ambra's comedy *La Cofanaria*, the performers approach from various sides and directions.[12] This information appears to be significant for understanding the musical performance of *intermedi*: because, accordingly, if the space of the stage was unconfined in these performances, the sound was also extending beyond, behind, above, and aside the stage, blurring the distinction between the spaces of the listener/observer and the performer. Indeed, in the first *intermedio* for *La Cofanaria*, we discover that eight voices were accompanied by musicians behind the stage, and that a scent was experienced during their performance.[13] The same happens in the second intermezzo, while in the fifth one, four horrible serpents emerge from the traps in which four violinists were concealed, and together with trombones behind the stage, they accompany Psyche's madrigal.[14] It seems that the sound that comes from afar, from different directions, or from the very stage but without apparent source was an important part of scenic illusion. Indeed, these "stereophonic effects," as Nino Pirrotta calls them, were a sonic equivalent of the elaborate machinery that was used to create a visual illusion. Pirrotta sees this phenomenon as a sixteenth-century "fondness for the sense of mystery created by the remoteness of instruments as well as by the obstructions which sweetened and veiled the sound," discovering that for

---

[11] Tim Carter points out Grazzini's lamenting of "la meraviglia, ohimè, degli intermedi." Tim Carter, "Intermedio," *Grove Music Online*, L. Macy (ed.), http://www.grovemusic.com (accessed January, 13 2008). But this remark can be found in almost every relevant reference book on music history.

[12] "Accordingly, a brief space after the descent of the curtains which conceal from the eyes of the Spectators the Perspective of the concave Heavens of the opening scene, there is seen to appear a second, most ingeniously contrived Heaven... At the same time there was seen at one extremity of the perspective, as though walking on the earth, Cupid approaching with wings and quite nude as he is described by poets... The first Act being finished, there is seen issuing, from one of the four passageways left between the scenes for the use of the actors, a tiny Cupid... etc." See: "Music at a Medici Wedding," in Piero Weiss and Richard Taruskin (eds), *Music in the Western World: A History in Documents* (New York: Schirmer Books, 1984), p. 115.

[13] A.M. Nagler, *Theatre Festivals of the Medici 1539–1637* (New Haven and London: Yale University Press, 1964), p. 18.

[14] Ibid., p. 20.

the inauguration of the *Teatro Olimpico* in Vicenza (1585), for example, at the beginning of the spectacle is heard: 'from behind the scenes, a music of instruments and voices, the sweetest possible, with a plaintive overall effect; and ... done so that it seems to resound from afar.'"[15] I believe, though, that these effects unveil more: the spatial configurations of performers and observers also evince a sense of the self that is not entirely separated from its surroundings, participating in the spectacle as a fundamentally communal illusion.

It would be convenient to relate this discussion on music and space to the sense of oftentimes discussed limitless space of Baroque art. It is enough to remind ourselves of Bernini's depiction of the rapture of St. Teresa, which includes not only the statue of the saint hovering on a cloud at the center of the piece, but also the painted representation of swarms of angels tumbling down from high above the altar, and, in addition, the supposed observers to the scene represented as if sitting in opera boxes overlooking the ecstatic display. The purpose of these imaginary viewers is to make a connection with the ones who really stand in front of what is represented, thereby creating an illusion that they too belong to the scene and testify to the miracle. These Baroque experimentations with "frames" and "confines" should be understood as tokens of the new awareness of a possible autonomous stage space. In other words, the autonomy of the theater stage was not achieved immediately but through a long process of exploration that involved various standards and rules of performance, as manifested in the spatial experiments of the Baroque. If Bernini's inclusion of possible observers blurs the boundaries between audience and centerpiece, it further complicates them in relation to the other parts of this complex installation: the depiction of angels that emerge from the light high above creates an illusion of the unreachable space that belongs to neither the stage nor the audience. The power of the illusion lies in the fact that the audience feels as if it is taking part in the miracle in which St. Teresa mediates between the earthly and the heavenly.

Music, however, is performative, and the spatial relationships in *intermedi*, even if sharing the characteristic of Baroque art that extends beyond the confines of representational frame, are very much bounded by the fact that they were a part of social ritual performed in time. *Intermedi* were a part of elaborate, sometimes weeks-long Florentine celebrations like wedding nuptials and state visits, and only one among various entertainments, including masquerades and banquets with music; jousts, tournaments, and pageants; mock battles, hunts, equestrian ballets, and *calcio* games.

In order to understand the expectations of audiences, it is not irrelevant to point at the interactive character of indoors court entertainments in general. Court ballets and tournaments, for example, could be stopped at any time, calling for active participation of the courtiers. In *veglias* and *mascheratas*, the *gradi* were

---

[15]   Nino Pirrotta, "Orchestra and Stage in Renaissance *Intermedi*," *Music and Culture in Italy from the Middle Ages to the Baroque* (Cambridge, Massachusetts, and London, England: Harvard University Press, 1984), p. 212.

erected on three sides, with a stage on the fourth side and a clear floor space left in between for dancing. The stage and auditorium were connected with ramps and staircases, and the stage performers could easily mingle with the courtiers.[16] "In these the ballet that began on stage overflowed the ramps into the auditorium, where a space on the floor was kept open for the development of a figured ballroom dance."[17] In the performance of the *veglia Notte d'amore* (1608), for example, the amoretti begin to dance, mingling with the spectators, and Cupid from the stage invites guests to continue dancing.[18]

From this perspective, in *intermedi*, as in other forms of courtly entertainment, the sense of space cannot be divorced from their performativity and social role. Unlike the spaces of church facades, monuments, and paintings, theirs is always the space of social performance, with an emphasis on its ritual dimension. And even if they share Baroque disrespect for the stage bounded by *prospettiva*, they are more significantly related to their temporal element whose imminent effect – the illusion that both symbolical (representational) and physical worlds come together – recreates a spatial and temporal transgression that here becomes a part of bodily experience, a recreation of an imagined world in the act of performance. As I will now demonstrate, the physical and the allegorical, the artistic illusion and collective catharsis, come together, negating spatial and temporal frames, and creating an unusual world of fantasy that is, in the first place, communal. The symbolic recreation of a macrocosm in time creates the space in which the self is immersed in the collective.

The *Intermedi* for *La Pellegrina*: Performing the Macrocosm

The first *intermedio* of *La Pellegrina* – performed at the 1589 wedding of Ferdinando de' Medici and Christine of Lorraine – displays a complex allegory of the harmony of the spheres: Dorian Harmony (*Armonia Doria*) descends on

---

[16]   The relationships of power are openly performed at these ceremonies. Pirrotta claims: "In spectacles whose action spilled over in the pit, the performers on stage tended to be separated from those in the pit by a class distinction, in that the latter were nobles, even the most noble among those present. One example is the *Ballo delle ingrate* (Mantua, 1608) by Rinuccini and Monteverdi, in which the performers in the pit were 'the duke and the betrothed prince, together with six cavaliers and eight ladies, chosen from among the most prominent of the city on the basis of nobility, beauty, and grace in dancing.' Another, with an even more pronounced distinction of rank, is (…) *Liberazione di Tirreno*: 'In the middle of the auditorium the grand duke danced amid cavaliers, and the archduchess amid ladies, yet with gestures and movements and placements that were always differentiated from those of the others, so that even though they all followed the same music, the masters were always recognized as such.'" Pirrotta, p. 213.

[17]   Nagler, p. 2.

[18]   Ibid., p. 101.

earth, together with other Harmonies, Sirens, Fates, and Planets, inviting humans to celebrate the bridal couple. First, Dorian Harmony emerges on a cloud from the skies and sings her madrigal, and then, after she wondrously disappears, the sirens, sitting on four hovering clouds show up to sing their tune, only to be followed by the emergence of three additional cloud-machines: the one at the center holding Necessity whose diamond spindle keeps the world going around, and Planets on the other two. The allegory becomes complete in the number *A Voi Reali Amanti* (*To You Royal Rulers*), which includes a reference to the Medici's power as the earthly equivalent of divine harmony. Although the majority of audience may not have recognized a subtle reference to Plato's *Republic* in this *intermedio*, the sources reveal that they all praised the splendor of stage scenery, lavish even by today's standards, with an artificial lightning, complex machinery, and performers sitting on clouds that miraculously emerge from all sides as if they are rising from earth and descending from skies.[19]

The dialogue between the Sirens and Fates was performed in a particular manner: while the Sirens address the newlyweds, they ascend on a cloud, singing: "So let us weave garlands for such great rulers, with flowers and friezes from Paradise … With the Sun and the Moon and wonders lovelier still." With these words, the Sirens ascend as if Paradise, Sun, and Moon are above the stage, just a hand's reach. The ascension of the Sirens leaves little doubt as to what the purpose of this stage maneuver is: it is a moment of bringing the heavens to mortals, the moment of symbolical link of the earthly and divine. Mythical characters address the Medici, thus making a connection between the past and present tangible. In the same way that earth and sky come together in the Uffizi palace, mythical and historical time become one uninterrupted line: Harmony, the Planets, the Fates, and the Medici – they are all the protagonists in this event. This connection is celebrated in the final *intermedio* when the gods, upon descending on earth, take the mortals by hand and teach them to dance.

This metaphorical representation of cosmic totality requires much more than simply obeying the rules of *prospettiva*, for how can the divine be limited by mere representation? So, it is not that perspective is somehow abandoned through the use of elaborate machinery that significantly jumps out of the stage frame in describing the link between the worlds. It is that visual illusion is not enough. As Panofsky points out, perspective negates the difference between front and back, between right and left, between bodies and intervening space.[20] And although modern theater rather early adopted perspective (*picture plane, looking though a section*

---

[19]   Nagler consults, among others, the sources by Bastiano de' Rossi, Giuseppe Pavoni, and Barthold von Gadenstedt in describing the disappearing act of Harmony: "Several sunbeams burst forth from behind the cloud, which was so altogether 'convincing' that the spectators were at a loss to say how it moved as it gradually floated to the earth, headed toward the temple, and then vanished into it, along with *Armonia Doria*." Ibid., p. 74.

[20]   Erwin Panofsky, *Perspective as Symbolic Form* (New York: Zone Books, 1991), p. 31.

cut from infinite space), the *intermedi* show that in performing arts the illusion does not have to be limited only to ocularcentric perspective. The illusionism in *La Pellegrina* creates the possibility of reaching outside of the circumscribed space, because its goal is not realistic representation, but exactly the opposite: bringing the ineffable to mortals.

We can only assume that the audience that required spectacle experienced the ascension in the moment of the utmost flattery addressed to the Medici as the allegory brought on a visceral level. The wonder of an echoing choir that floats in the air materializes, if only for a moment, the connection between the divine and human: and if the world exists as the harmony of the spheres, the Medici, imitating the divine through this amazing spectacle, rightfully appear to become its representatives on earth.

Sound Reflections, Traces of the Self

The storyline of *La Pellegrina* reveals an ethical understanding of music according to which a well-balanced universe depends on the fine tuning of its sounds. In other words, the way music is, influences all spheres of human existence. This Platonic concept, together with the use of the pastoral idiom as the scenic metaphor for worldly accord, is one among many revived ancient ideals in *La Pellegrina*. Almost every element in *intermedi* could be seen as a humanist recasting of ancient models, including fully developed *prospettivas* for the performing stage. And the most important innovation, the use of monody – soloist performance with an accompaniment of *basso continuo* that emphasized the meaning of text and ultimately led to the creation of opera – was inspired by another reimagining of how ancient Greeks and Romans performed their dramas.

It is echoing, though – a sonic symbol of the relationship between the human and nature – that becomes the favorite pastoral trope of ancient origins in this and other early modern works.[21] If the *intermedi* for *La Pellegrina* explore the power of music through the very medium of music, the use of echo becomes even more interesting. For what is an echo? It is sound that bounces back; the sound that delineates the borders and confines what it can or cannot reach. It is a psychophysical manifestation of the distance between the human being and its surroundings, an empirical exploration of spatial existence performed in sound.

---

[21] Fredrick W. Sternfeld traced, in several publications, the history of the trope of echoing from Euripides to T.S. Eliot. In early modern context, he cites two important influences for the development of echo poetry: Angelo Poliziano's *Miscellanea* (1489) and Giovan Battista Guarini's *Il Pastor Fido* (1590). Guarini's work had especially significant influence on composers. For further investigation, see Frederick W. Sternfeld, "Repetition and Echo in Renaissance Poetry and Music," *English Renaissance Studies, Presented to Dame Helen Gardner in honor of her Seventeenth Birthday* (New York: Oxford University Press, 1980), pp. 33–43.

Indeed, almost every pioneering work of modern musical drama contained a pastoral echo scene, beginning with what is today considered as the first attempt at opera – *Dafne* (1598), by Jacopo Peri and Ottavio Rinuccini.

It is no coincidence that the German polymath Athanasius Kircher (1601–1680) wrote an entire study on the phenomenon of echoing, creating a theoretical equivalent of experiments in music performance. Spending most of his life at the Roman College, the Jesuit Kircher compiled a vast body of knowledge in about 30 books. He entitled his work on echoing *Phonosophia Anacamptica*, "the knowledge of reflected sound" and published it on two occasions: the first time, as a part of his monumental study on music *Musurgia Universalis* (Romae: ex typographia haeredum Francisci Corbelletti, 1650), and the second time, in a more elaborate version in his work entitled *Phonurgia Nova* (Campidonœ: per Rudolphum Dreherr,1673).

Kircher was fascinated by echoing sound as an acoustic phenomenon, seeing in it an aural equivalent to light reflection in optics, and yet always emphasizing its interpretative fluidity by finding correspondences between its nature and the ancient myth of Echo, "the unfortunate pursuer" of Narcissus. He opens the preface to *Phonosophia*:

> The echo, that jest of Nature when she is in a playful mood, is called the 'image of a voice' by the poets, in accordance with that well-known line of Virgil's: *The rocks resound and the image of the voice that has struck them bounces back.* It is called a reflected, rebounding and alternating voice by scientists and 'the daughter of the voice' by the Israelites.[22]

As an early modern erudite, Kircher was interested in basically every manifestation of human activity and creation. The recent renaissance of his work lies precisely in his ability to assume correspondences between various spheres of human cognition, never dismissing the fact that one and the same phenomenon can (or even must) perpetuate numerous meanings and interpretations. This is how his elaborate study of echoing sound brings together acoustics, geometry, empirical and experimental research, myth, and poetry.[23] In the preface, he continues to explain his multifaceted research approach to the phenomenon of echoing:

> Such is its mysterious nature that up to this very day there is scarcely anyone who has explained it. It is indeed known, and is almost common knowledge, that it is a reflected voice, but how it is produced, from what sources, how it is spread, with what speed and over what distance, is as unknown as any phenomenon. It

---

[22]   Athanasius Kircher, "Phonosophia Anacamptica," Liber I in *Phonurgia nova, sive Conjugium mechanico-physicum artis & natvrœ paranympha phonosophia concinnatum…* (Campidonœ: per Rudolphum Dreherr, 1673), p. 1.

[23]   Kircher combines scientific method of axioms, hypothesis, and experiments with Euclidian form of definitions, propositions, and corollaries.

seems impossible to work through the immensity of the difficulties that one encounters unless, equipped with the greatest practical knowledge and unique diligence, one finally succeeds in tricking and catching this runaway Nymph with acts of wondrous skill. Since nobody hitherto has achieved this, in my desire to investigate it I have left nothing untried in my examination of the hidden recesses of forests, wooded glades and mountains, the hidden retreats of valleys, areas of stone rubble and plains, and the uncultivated flat areas of marshes, in order that I might come to grips with her hidden nature. [24]

Kircher's belief that everything in the knowing world has a correspondence obviously strongly influences not only his argument but also his style of argumentation. The elusive character of an ancient myth mirrors the indefinable nature of echoing, and everything else in relation to it, including our knowledge of it. The correspondence between the myth of Echo and Kircher's formidable pursuit becomes salient in Kircher's description:

> But as I pursue her, she runs away, while I run away, she pursues me, and she redoubles her voices by taking on additional voices like attendants, as she seductively tricks me and I cry out aloud, for she is incapable of yielding. At times, as though angry, she turns away and stealthily shuns any reply, at other times with a most ill-mannered talkativeness she pours out ten further words in reply to one word of mine.

In this context, the sound reflection is simultaneously magic, art, and science.[25] His understanding of these terms, of course, would not be as conflicted as ours today. Nonetheless, observed phenomena for Kircher always carry multiple significations. His work on echo is basically a study of sound reflections (what today we would call, in very general terms, sound waves) – in relation to the angles of their dissemination, the material and shape of the instruments that produce them, and the architecture of spaces in which they are created.[26] The fact that he bases his study of acoustics on the notion of echo, however, is proof of the empirical spirit in which knowledge does not originate from some kind of abstract

---

[24] Ibid.

[25] The first definition in his preface is: "The Sorcery, or Science of Voice-reflection is a more obscure branch of the knowledge of sounds, by which, through the power of the reflected and multiplied voice, we give produce effects that are amazing and, to those ignorant of the causes, miraculous." Ibid., p. 3.

[26] In the fourth section of the *Phonosophia*, besides referring to ancient sources (Vitruvius' writing on Corinthian theater), he also writes about echo phenomena in various architectonic structures that he examined, including Villa Simonetti, the grottos at the Syracuse prison (*auris Dionysii*), circular courtyards in Mantua and Caprarola, in addition to constant referring, throughout his study, to other architectonic spaces of his time, including Vatican Palace.

speculation, but it develops from human experience. It is a theoretical equivalent of experiments in music performance.

Self as a Character, the World as a Stage

In *La Pellegrina* the space of nature is already contained in the totality of spatial denotation: the Uffizi Theater becomes all the spaces at once. And the echoing becomes almost a temporary monument to the grandeur of the Uffizi and the ruling family. But this is not the only use of echo in this spectacle. Musicologist Nina Treadwell showed that the notation for the first song from the first *intermedio* also suggests a conclusion in an echoing manner: Harmony would sing her song, and her final words would be repeated from the other end of the hall.[27] And the fifth *intermedio* with the song of a mythical singer Arion lost at the sea contains elaborate echo effects that had to be performed with voices echoing from various sides.

In accord with this variety of echo effects, the *intermedi* for *La Pellegrina* also offer formal diversity, containing both traditional madrigals like the one by Malvezzi and the stylistic innovations of monodies like in Arion's song by Malvezzi's student Jacopo Peri. Although Arion's song *Dunque fra torbide onde* (Thus over troubled waters) describes the same sense of spatial illusion – Arion is lost at the sea, and he laments his ordeal while the vast space of the sea shore echoes his voice back – his musical rhetoric is quite different. In comparison to the echoes of the Sirens and the Planets, written in a traditional form of a choral madrigal, Arion's song brings about the mastery of soloist performance in long and elaborated coloraturas, much more similar to the introductory song of Harmony. Originally, both Harmony's and Arion's songs were performed by Florentine stars: Vittoria Archilei and Jacopo Peri, excellent singers and composers.[28] While Harmony's rhetorical ability is understood as inherent and all encompassing in its allegorical representation of a ruling life principle, however, Arion's is the rhetoric of a mythical singer, whose character guides the dramatic and musical action. In other words, Arion expresses his personal feelings caused by a very specific series of events.[29]

---

[27] Nina Treadwell, "Changing Time: Temporal Perceptions in Medician Musical Theater," presented at the 2004–2005 Clark conference core program *Structures of Feeling in Seventeenth-Century Cultural Expression* directed by Susan McClary, William Andrews Clark Memorial Library, May 20, 2005.

[28] While it's quite sure that Peri composed his song, Nina Treadwell suggested that Vittoria Archilei as a performer probably had a significant input in creation of *La Pellegrina*'s opening number. See Nina Treadwell, "She descended on a cloud 'from the highest spheres:' Florentine Monody 'alla Romanina'," *Cambridge Opera Journal*, 16/1 (2004): pp. 1–22.

[29] According to a legend, Arion, was on his way back home to Corinth, after winning a singing competition in Sicily. The sailors decided to take away his valuable awards and get rid of him.

And what about the space? Arion is not entirely separated from the audience. His song, in the same way as the madrigal of the Planets and the Fates, bounces back, simulating the illusionary space of an open sea, in which the audience is caught in between Arion's echoes as if they are witnessing his desolation. "Gentle Echo with your gentle accents, redouble my torments," sings Arion. Peri uses a doubling effect to emphasize Arion's sadness, repeating his sighs and the words that signify suffering and grief. The purpose of the echo is to magnify these affects and present them as an aural hallucination to which the Medici's guests would succumb. The repetitiveness of expressive phrases emphasizes singer's rhetorical prowess and overwhelms the listener's senses with the vertigo of multiplying auditory affects. Although it participates in the same spatial illusionism created by echoing that I discussed in relation to the scene with Harmony, the Planets, and the Fates, Arion's song reveals a sense of uniqueness and distinctive characterization that is brought about precisely by his rhetorical prowess. If Planets and Fates echo each other in order to symbolize heavenly powers, Arion makes out of echo a display of his own power, for indeed, in the end, he gets saved by the dolphins touched by his beautiful song.

Arion is, obviously, not just any character: like Orpheus, he is a manipulator of human passions whose power lies in his control of the listeners; a character that was easily appropriated by musicians as a metaphorical representation of their own creative empowerment and ability. At this point, a metaphysical concept of creation gets weakened and the mythical singer becomes the representative of the human divine: the possibility to create and imitate the perfection of nature. It is hardly a coincidence that Peri came up with this idea: he was already famous for his music activity, and was seen as an innovative musician, not only because of his performing skills but also because of new music ideas.[30]

This is not to say that Arion's monody is the first display of subjectivity in early modern music. In her study *Modal Subjectivities: Self-Fashioning in the Italian Madrigal*, Susan McClary demonstrated that already "from around 1525 the Italian madrigal serves as a site … for the explicit, self-conscious construction *in*

---

[30] Pietro de' Bardi, the son of Giovanni de' Bardi, described Peri's presence in the Florentine circle his father gathered: "Also in Florence at this time was Jacopo Peri, who, as the first pupil of Cristofano Malvezzi, received high praise as a player of the organ and the keyboard instruments and as a composer of counterpoint, and he was rightly regarded as second to none of the singers in that city. This man, in competition with Giulio (Caccini), brought the enterprise of the *stile rappresentativo* to light, and avoiding a certain roughness, and excessive antiquity that had been felt in the compositions of Galilei (Vincenzo), he, together with Giulio, sweetened this style and made it capable of moving the affections in a rare manner, as in the course of time was done by them both. " Pietro de' Bardi: "Letter to Giovanni Battista Doni," in Leo Treitler (ed.), *Source Readings in Music History*, (New York: W.W. Norton & Company, 1998), p. 524.

music of subjectivities."[31] Further, Nino Pirrotta demonstrated that even madrigals went though the change in perspective, from expressing the feelings of an abstract subject to those of a very specific character: "For some time the madrigalists had tended to abandon merely lyrical expression (in which text and music express, or seem to express, subjective feelings) and had begun to represent sentiments attributed to fictitious characters."[32] Arion's scene in *La Pellegrina*, however, involves both solo performance and stage illusion that significantly enhance dramatic verisimilitude of a described situation – a future guiding force of opera as *drama in musica*.

"The world as a stage" starts to exist exactly in the moment when the "stage" and the "world" become deeply separated, and yet this profound separation begins to define existence in both realms: stage imitates life and life becomes staged. But, as we saw, in *intermedi*, the world hasn't quite become a stage yet: the protagonists are usually allegorical representations of mythical figures, virtues, and abstract principles, and only occasionally – characters. Arion's echoing song, however, demonstrates a transition, unveiling a characterization whose model will be imitated in various musical stage works throughout early modernity. In other words, the *intermedi* reflect a transitory moment in the history of spectacle, caught in between its premodern understanding, in which a microcosm is still immersed in the totality of macrocosm, and its modern counterpart – a display of the character on the stage as the representation of modern self, strongly separated from the audience and constantly under the silent inspection of their gaze.[33]

Paradigm changes, though, are never clear-cut and all encompassing. The stream led by Peri did become more influential: for the wedding of Henri

---

[31]   Susan McClary, *Modal Subjectivities: Self-Fashioning in the Italian Madrigal* (Berkeley: University of California Press, 2004), p. 6. Over the two last decades, a relevant body of scholarship, including McClary's, has broken through the years-old prejudice about music as an ineffable art whose transcendental potentials go beyond explication, let alone quite definable social and cultural meanings. Early modern composers made extensive use of various musical techniques that explore changes in human perception in ways that resemble those recorded in contemporaneous visual imagery.

[32]   Pirrotta, "Temperaments and Tendencies in the Florentine Camerata," p. 220.

[33]   This aspect of my work was influenced by the writings of William Egginton. In theater theory, Egginton defines the premodern notion of spectacle as *presence* and the modern as *theatricality*. According to Egginton, *presence* is evoked in any kind of ritual where the entire community participates in the performing process, "that experience of space that subtends such diverse experiences as the participation in a ritual invocation of the seasons, certain shamanistic cures, 'voodoo death,' and the miracle of transubstantiation," while *theatricality* defines modern stage rituals divided between the space of observer (listener) and the space of character (performer). He also influenced my use of the word *spectacle* (instead of more common – the *theater*) when discussing both premodern and modern musical practices. For further discussion, see William Egginton, *How the World Became a Stage: Presence, Theatricality and the Question of Modernity* (Albany: State University of New York, 2003), especially pp. 67–85.

IV and Maria de' Medici in 1600, Jacopo Peri and Ottavio Rinuccini created *Euridice*, the first opera to survive complete.[34] Its experimental nature, though, was somewhat academically dry for aristocratic Florentines, who enjoyed traditional entertainments.[35] That is why, in 1608, on the first celebratory occasion following the first operatic experiment, *intermedi* were back as the main source of entertainment. And opera took on a new life, outside of the city it originated from, but strongly related to the issues raised in its Florentine beginnings.

As exemplified in the previous discussion, my intention is to show that both the creation and deconstruction of the musical canon had to do with changes in the perception of space. By the end of the seventeenth and beginning of the eighteenth centuries, the simulation of spatiality had become incorporated and "framed" into the musical work, which, in terms of visual perspective, became stage-centered. In this context, it would be easy to assume that the de-centered performances of *intermedi* maintain premodern conceptions of space: in these performances, as in medieval drama and visual art, there is more than one focus of the spectator's gaze, and one's visual attention becomes scattered in different directions.

I believe, however, that precisely this negotiation between off-stage and on-stage spaces (the experimentation with centered perspective and limits of the stage) reflects the new awareness of the difference between the two and defines the conscience of modern audience. In other words, I define the dialectics of spatial closure and openness as a historical phenomenon that gains relevance exactly at the moment when the stage becomes a separate space for the theatrical display of imaginary innerness, while the other space, the space of the audience, becomes deeply separated from what is represented on the scene. It is Jacopo Peri, the singer, who takes the character of Arion while performing. But as have I shown in my discussion, *intermedi* offered to the audience both contemplation/observation and participation; they belong to a genre that simultaneously reflects two different concepts of space.

But once the stage space became autonomous, the emotions of imaginary characters with whom the audience could chose to identify (or not) became the core of dramatic representation.[36] Here I again emphasize the relevance of the

---

[34] We can say little about *Il Rapimento di Cefalo*, another opera performed for this occasion, with music by Giulio Caccini and libretto by Gabrielo Chiabrera: most of its music is lost, with only the text and accounts of its performance preserved.

[35] Tim Carter explains various reasons for opera's apparent "failure" in Florence. In the first place, he mentions overall deficiencies of the performance, but he also points out at the significant competition between Giovanni de'Bardi and Emilio de' Cavalieri, the two masterminds of Florentine spectacles. Bardi was apparently very critical of the new recitative style displayed in *Euridice*. And since his power in Florence significantly declined at this point, this critique was even more poignant. See: Tim Carter, "A Florentine wedding of 1608," *Acta Musicologica*, vol. 55, Fasc. 1 (Jan.–Jun., 1983): p. 93.

[36] Nino Pirrotta claims that even madrigals went though this change in perspective: "For some time the madrigalists had tended to abandon merely lyrical expression (in which

historical moment: towards the end of the sixteenth century, representation becomes crucial in music, and this paradigm shift, so well exemplified in the discussion between Monteverdi and Artusi, forever changed the discursive features of the modern musical canon. Thus if music, as well as other arts, in premodern time *resembled* the world (to use Foucault's category), now it started to *signify* it: if premodern musical performances sonically embodied the harmony of the spheres or unity with God, on the modern stage the sounds stood as representations of these expressions (or, more accurately, affects) that the audience could identify with or ignore, according to their opinions or tastes. This division between the emotion and its representation is what so strongly offended Artusi's belief in the magic powers of music.

I already have shown that the production of *intermedi* is both similar to and different from that of opera; after all, it is not a coincidence that discussions of this genre conclude historical surveys on Renaissance music or begin Baroque ones, explaining it as a predecessor to opera – a "real" modern musical invention. The truth, however, is that *intermedi* stayed well into the seventeenth century as a favorite musical genre at Italian courts. While opera struggled, finally finding its refuge in liberal-minded and market-oriented Venice, *intermedi* flourished throughout the majority of Italian regions; and precisely, I believe, because of their specific understanding of the performing space.[37]

Echoing Labyrinths of the Self

Previously, I showed how Arion's echoing voice represents the power of a singer capable of performing so beautifully that he can save himself from certain death (in one version of the myth, the dolphins save Arion after hearing his beautiful song). His embellished lamentation, however, seems rather simple in comparison to Claudio Monteverdi's uses of echo in his *favola in música*, *L'Orfeo* (1607). Firstly, Monteverdi exploits the metaphor of echoing in Orfeo's central aria "Possente spirito:" in order to persuade the gods to return his beloved Euridice from the dead, Orfeo puts to work all his rhetorical skills, and Monteverdi magnifies the height of Orfeo's rhetorical potency with exuberant instrumental echoes of his melismatic vocal melody. Both Peri and Monteverdi use the echo effect as the manifestation

---

text and music express, or seem to express, subjective feelings) and had begun to represent sentiments attributed to fictitious characters." Pirrotta, "Temperaments and Tendencies in the Florentine Camerata," p. 220.

[37]   Ellen Rosand demonstrates how the operas created in Florence, Mantua, and Rome have a strong resemblance to the court music tradition of *intermedi*. She claims that the history of Venetian public opera is the beginning of the genre as we know it today. See Ellen Rosand, *Opera in Seventeenth-Century Venice: The Creation of a Genre* (Berkeley: University of California Press, 1991).

of the resounding auditory power of mythical musicians empowered with awe-inspiring performing skills.

Monteverdi, however, goes further and presents the antithesis to this rhetorical abundance in the conclusion to his opera. As Orfeo laments after losing Euridice, the concluding syllables of each phrase are thrown back at him. Aggravated by Echo's restrained responses, Orfeo sings: *Courteous loving Echo, you who are disconsolate, and wish to console me in my anguish ... while I complain, alas, why do you answer me only with final accents?*[38] Bitter, lost, and powerless, Orfeo becomes deprived of his expressive abilities; the short answers of Echo embody his rhetorical lack.

Both Peri and Monteverdi use echo to describe the feeling of inner torment, but Monteverdi transforms the simple effect used in Peri's *Dunque fra torbide onde*. In "Possente spirito," the echo "translates" into a composing principle: while the voice sings, the instruments (first bowed strings, then wind, and finally plucked strings) elaborate previously vocal musical thoughts. However, while we know that Peri's aria was performed with singers responding from various parts of the performing hall, it is not clear what kind of performing manner Monteverdi had in mind for "Possente spirito."[39] Whether performed in one way or another, in Monteverdi's aria, Arion's vocal echoes were transformed into instrumental embellished melismas in keeping with Orfeo's reputation as both a powerful singer and a virtuoso lyre player.

Orfeo's echoing sighs in the opera's final act depict quite a different dramatic situation than the instrumental echoes of rhetoric prowess in "Possente spirito." To compose a beautiful lamentation and then reinforce its affectation through repeating echoes seems to be one of the favorite rhetorical tropes in many early modern works, including Giacomo Carissimi's *Jephte* and Biagio Marini's *La Bella Erminia*. There are other seventeenth-century settings of the Orpheus myth, like Stefano Landi's *Morte d'Orpheo*, which continue to use this effect. Upon a closer look into the history of rhetoric, the relationship between Orpheus and the trope of echoing, and especially the connection between lamentation and echoing, is a long-lasting one. Frederick Sternfeld points out that even Ovid inherited and accepted manners of lamentation from older sources, that is, from his Greek

---

[38] *Cortese Eco amorosa che sconsolata sei, e consolar mi vuoi ne' dolor miei,. Ma mentr'io mi querelo deh, perché mi rispondi sol con gl'ultimi accenti?*

[39] And the instruments were placed in the Mantuan performance, as we find out, in the orchestra pit, not in an offstage space. "The solution destined to prevail – placing the instruments in the foot of the stage, where they could see the singers and be seen by them, while a partition rendered them invisible to the spectators – was arrived at with difficulty. I believe that it have been tried for the first time in Mantua in 1607, when Monteverdi's *L'Orfeo* was presented 'su angusta scena' (on a constricted stage). This spectacle, which had to be given in a long narrow hall, thus impelling lateral placement of the musicians behind the scenes, forced the creation of an intermediate area between the stage and the auditorium which today we call orchestra pit." Pirrotta, p. 214.

predecessors. Sternfeld claims that Ovid passed on to the Renaissance not only the subject matter from the Greek mythology but also their modes of expression. In this context, lamentation was traditionally represented by repetition and echoing.[40] This manner of lamentation can be already found in Euripides's *Andromeda*, where the heroine laments her faith while echoes bounce back.[41] In the conclusion to *Orfeo*, Monteverdi only masterfully used one of the conventional rhetorical figures in musical-poetical representation of grief.[42]

I will now look at pieces that go beyond the traditional use of echo as lament, and whose creators even more significantly experiment with a display of echo as a musical *maniera*, while negotiating between the sense of presence and theatricality. Earlier in this chapter, I emphasized the famous example of the echo song by Lasso because its zesty aspect becomes relevant for the rhetoric of other sixteenth- and seventeenth-century echo music, including the piece that will be at the center of my discussion in following pages: Biagio Marini's *Sonata in Ecco* for three violins (1629). Marini's sonata exhibits the full range of complex meanings that the rhetoric of echo developed in early modern music, including both the simple thrill with the possibilities of musical representation and, as its final result, the overwhelming of sensory perception.

Marini very often moved from place to place, working at various Catholic courts. He was one among many Italian composers who moved beyond the Alps,

---

[40]   Sternfeld elaborated this claim in: Frederick W. Sternfeld, "Orpheus, Ovid and Opera," *Journal of the Royal Musical Association*, vol.113, no.2 (1988): pp. 172–202.

[41]   Ibid., p. 178.

[42]   We find the same manner of lamentation still fashionable in 1724 in Antonio Vivaldi's *Il Giustino*. Vivaldi uses a historical background of Byzantium to tell a conventionally complicated and rather mundane story of *opera seria*, whose dramatic labyrinths of turns and twists unmistakingly culminate in a happy end. The five characters go through a series of dramatic events that perpetually complicate and postpone the solution to the drama: the Byzantine emperor Anastasio is threatened by Vitalino who wants to take his throne and his wife Arianna; the other story line involves a common ploughman Giustino who dreams of a military glory and, upon meeting the emperor's sister Leocasta manages to prove himself as a warrior and, by the end of the opera, even to advance to the status of an emperor. Gods, terrible monsters, lightning bolts and ghostly voices all appear to enhance the grandeur of the spectacle. One of the tricks that belong to the same category of bedazzling the audience is the use of echo. At the beginning of the second act, rejected Vitalino punishes Arianna by chaining her to the rock and leaving her to the mercy of a terrible monster. Arianna cries for help and her cries are doubled in echoes. Nothing could be further from Vivaldi's spectacle, however, than Cristoph Willibald Gluck's use of echoing in his version of Orfeo's myth (*Orfeo ed Euridice*, 1762, Italian version). Gluck simplifies the dramatic action: the instrumental offstage echoes of a choir and Orfeo's aria in the first act of the opera deny spectacle-like qualities; they serve as a simple, yet emotional reiteration of lamentation. This is the first time that echo seems integrated in musical structure in a way that it more significantly reflects mood or inner state than spatial relationship. It almost becomes the musical abstraction of a physical phenomenon.

propagating new musical styles to the rest of Europe. He probably composed this sonata while staying at Neuberg, a small town deep inside Bavaria, the residence of the Bavarian ruling family, the Wittelsbachs. His engagement shows how Italian art and music easily conquered northern European regions, internationalizing Italian trends.

Marini was no doubt familiar with the dramatic uses of echo in the vocal music of his time. He took on a quite different challenge, however, when incorporating this rhetoric figure into the purely instrumental genre of the sonata, without the help of narrative contextualization. Marini had a different purpose in mind: the violin's full potential still waited to be explored, and he used echoing in order to advance this project. The *Sonata in Ecco* reveals how the early developmental stages of the sonata were modeled on the textures of vocal music: in this piece, it is often easy to imagine the three violins replaced by three voices; on the other hand, this sonata's numerous displays of technical virtuosity obviously reinforce the instrumental nature of the genre. Marini imagined his *Sonata in Ecco* as the act of a performer at work: the subject is actually the performer who has discovered a new toy (an instrument) and wants to examine its capacities. As a successful violinist who pioneered various virtuosic effects on this instrument, Marini chose to posit the performing act as a way of exploring innerness.

Marini plays with the three-part structure of his sonata, concluding every section with elaborate echo effects that significantly change musical meanings. Every expressive exposition of the solo violin becomes disturbed with instrumental echoing from off stage. The second and third violins should play *sempre piano* from a place where they cannot be seen by the audience, recommends Marini at the very beginning of the score. They should repeat, from behind the scenes, the motives of the first violin.

In the first section, one can sense a certain pleasure in the echoing passages, as Marini merely indulges with childlike enthusiasm in the game of echoing. The first repetition is based on a rather simple passage motive. The second motive becomes more interesting, with elaborated trills, as if the performer liked the effect made by the first one. Then, the first violin plays with its own supposed echo, doubling the melody in thirds, creating the illusion of "catching" its own reflection and playing with it as with its own "thoughts." Marini shows how the thrill of the new game develops with every new trick, something that Lasso had exploited in his *Echo song*. This naïveté in the *Sonata in Ecco*, though, has in particular to do with the discovery of the self. Marini, an embodiment of *homo ludens*, realizes through this echo-simulation the kinds of marvelous artifice is he able to create. Hauser wonderfully describes the same effect in mannerist art:

> a mannerist work of art is always a piece of bravura, a triumphant conjuring trick, a firework display with flying sparks and colours. The effect depends on the defiance of the instinctual, the naively natural and rational, and the emphasis laid on the obscure, the problematical, and the ambiguous, the incomplete nature of the manifest which points to its opposite, the latent, the missing link

in the chain. Beauty too beautiful becomes unreal, strength too strong becomes acrobatics, too much content loses all meaning, form independent of content becomes an empty shell.[43]

Could we label Marini's echo game as *maniera* or as *affetto*? The visceral character of music makes this distinction between intellectual mannerism and the emotional Baroque difficult to make. There is something of both in Marini: the musical structure based on the fascination with space, on one side, and emotional exhaustion with the game, on the other. The distinction will be clearer once we get into another seventeenth-century piece at the very end of this section.

As previously described, Arion's and Orfeo's echoes are reflections of their emotional states. The two singers not only sing their sorrow, but through echoing, they become aware of it and able to recognize its impact. This aspect of self-recognition becomes very important for Marini's purely instrumental genre. If the performer in his sonata at first naively listens to his own echo, he later becomes entranced by his own reverberation and tries to create new phrases that can thrill him as they bounce back. In the second part, Marini further develops little tricks from the first section: the first violin plays double stops, and the violins from the background readily respond; furthermore the soloist plays with syncopations, new and old passages, and broken chords. The performer's interest in a newly discovered game reaches its pinnacle at this point. This aural self-reflection again could be explained by visual metaphor: when standing in front of the mirror while holding another mirror against it, one sees multiple reflections of the self (holding a mirror) at the point where the two mirrors intersect. Marini translates this spatial metaphor into the temporality of music: the violinist hears his own sound reflections, then becomes influenced by them and creates new sounds that somehow respond to the preceding ones. It is the sonic equivalent of a visual representation of "a picture within a picture" or "a reflection within a reflection," so popular in mannerist art.

What is really interesting, though, is how Marini ends his sonata. The phrases at this point become very short: the performer stops and listens to the reverb on every tone of the D major chord – the penultimate sonority before the expected resolution to the sonata's tonic, G. But instead of finishing on the tonic G that would successfully conclude the piece, the resounding of a tense D from the violins in the background lingers on – and that's the end. Perpetual echoing on a high-strung chord does not satisfactorily conclude the piece, no matter how the violinists choose to perform it. If performed energetically, the final measures communicate unceasing enthusiasm: an effect that would be even more emphasized if the performing venue has lively reverberation. If the violinists decide to end the piece in decrescendo (the performing manner I'm more inclined to), they convey a certain boredom with the whole enterprise. In both cases, the long stop on the suspenseful

---

[43]   Arnold Hauser, *Mannerism: The Crisis of the Renaissance and the Origin of Modern Art*, trans. Eric Mosbacher (Cambridge: Harvard University Press, 1986), p. 13.

chord represents the impossibility of concluding the piece in a "proper" way. By doing this, Marini challenges the possibilities of the musical trope of echoing more extravagantly than his predecessors. His inconclusive indulgence in auditory self-reflection conveys not only self-empowerment, but also bewilderment with indefinite resounding. Unable to conclude the piece, Marini projects a self that, in one way or another, becomes lost in the labyrinths of its own reflections.

Marini's sonata simulates a kind of excitement with oneself: the very notion of being able to listen to one's own thoughts arouses emotions; the echoing phrase returns unchanged, but hearing it again creates a fascination with one's own creativity and a desire to come up with a new idea and then another. What about the ending, then? I have already mentioned that the effect of "fading out" does not make for very convincing closure, especially since it is tonally unstable. The result is not the opening up of the structure to new developments, but some kind of emotional stasis in which the game ends when the excitement quails. The final never-ending chord depicts what happens when curiosity becomes satisfied. It echoes boredom. The subject in front of the mirror, like Narcissus confronted with his own image, is finally always alone.

Sonata in Ecco shows how the effect of limitless space signified by echoing "merges" into the sonata's formal and affective structure. The echo effect entirely shapes the logic and dramaturgy of the piece. At this point, the physical space is of equal importance to the autonomous space of the piece, and they unavoidably influence each other: the fascination with the limitless space creates a limitless (unconcluded) musical structure.

In my examples thus far, the echo effect represents a forceful articulation of labyrinthine interiority that is exploring the sense of the self in its surroundings. To be able to find the way out of labyrinth is to be capable of reaching a goal and resolving one's own destiny and that seems to be the most difficult goal, especially in Marini's piece. Labyrinth – an important metaphor in mannerist aesthetics and in early modern culture – signifies the sense of uncertain existence, paradox and conflict. Gustav René Hocke explains that the "labyrinth-motive" becomes especially relevant in the culture and art of sixteenth- and seventeenth-century Europe, as well as in the later period, between the years of 1880 and 1950.[44] Hauser uses this metaphor in explaining a mannerist work of art as "a labyrinth [in which] you lose yourself and do not seek to escape from."[45]

In another seventeenth-century piece, *Saul, Saul was verfolgst du mich?* (*Saul, Saul, why do you persecute me?*, 1650), Heinrich Schütz transforms the rhetorical device of echoing into a swirling metaphor of auditory persecution that very much resembles Hauser's vision; the vocal echo effects depict the almighty voice that torments Saul. Strongly influenced by Italian Counter-Reformation art, Schütz creates a piece that negotiates the irreparable sense of self-guilt – a

[44] Gustav René Hocke, *Die Welt als Labyrinth: Manier und Manie in der Europäischen Kunst* (Hamburg: Rowohlt, 1957), p. 101.

[45] Hauser, p. 25.

Leitmotive of Protestant doctrine – with all the theatrical emotional affectations of the Catholic Baroque. In this piece, echoing displays an emotionally charged affect that cannot be compared to mannerist detachment. The horror is palpable and overtly expressed – the very essence of the Baroque according to Panofsky, which is "humanly simple" or "simply human."[46]

The conclusion of Schütz's piece raises similar issues as Marini's sonata. The question at the very end – "why do you persecute me?" – might be posed differently, as Schütz shows early on in the piece; it can be asked by the entire ensemble, reflecting Saul's agony at its peak. Instead, the piece ends with the title question quietly sung by two soloists, simulating the emotional and physical numbness caused by the auditory hallucination. Interestingly, Saul's voice never sounds in this piece, but only the multiple voices of his assailant. However, "the lack of subject" in this case creates quite an opposite effect: it is the listener who hears with the ears of Saul, surrounded by the surreal auditory attack. Schütz creates this immediate effect by using a large performing ensemble (soloists, two choirs and violins) on one hand, and a minimal narrative content of only two textual phrases on the other. The discrepancy is not obvious, but it would be logical to expect that Schütz might have chosen such a large ensemble in order to depict a wide array of different musical effects. Instead, he focuses only on the representation of auditory persecution. He makes the first choice in order to achieve the monumental sound that properly depicts the wrath of God. But more importantly for this discussion, he uses the choirs and soloists to depict the effect of a voice moving through space in an echoing manner, which he learned from Italian composers. In this context, his strategy of using a minimal number of words becomes clearer: when the line *Saul, Saul, why do you persecute me?* repeatedly "travels" from bass to cantus, the listener becomes caught in the effect, experiencing what Saul supposedly experienced when falling to the ground struck by Jesus's voice. Another phrase, *It will become hard for you to kick against the thorns* (*Es wird dir schwer warden, wider den Stachel zu lökken*) is a direct threat to Saul that further deepens the emotional effect of fear and distress. Although in the New Testament Saul readily answers back (*Who are you, Lord*), in the motet, Schütz leaves him voiceless, choosing to describe and emphasize the powerful moment of Saul's emotional state in the moment of divine recognition. Schütz achieves the feeling of an overwhelming powerlessness of the subject (the listener, Saul) by means of the labyrinth of repeating voices: the phrases bounce off each other and none of them leads towards emotional relief. This sense of tortured subjectivity becomes a trademark of early modern art. This sense of disorientation leads us back to the metaphor of labyrinth. As Gustav René Hocke puts it, "One experienced the world

---

[46] Panofsky, Erwin. "What is Baroque?" *Three Essays on Style*, ed. Irving Lavin (Cambridge, MA: The MIT Press, 1997), p. 25.

as God's poetic labyrinth. But one no longer sought the entrance, or even only the exit. One remained stuck in the inextricable."[47]

Today, early modern echo pieces reveal very similar explorations of selfhood as the early modern examples of self-portraiture do: they reflect various ways of self-exploration in relation to the surrounding world. While in early examples, the effect of auditory mirroring has the dimension of an optimistic exploration of an entire new world of subjective experience, later examples bring about a certain doubt in the possibilities and limits of personal agency; they communicate the feeling of subject's destabilization and amazement at the impossibility of grasping the limits of being.

In eighteenth- and nineteenth-century music, the metaphor of echoing loses its cultural prominence, but never completely disappears from the repertoire. On the contrary, the imitation of spatiality in nineteenth-century symphonic music and, more significantly, in the dramatic effects on the opera stage are linked up with this tradition.[48] However, the spatiality of nineteenth and most of eighteenth century music is of a different kind; it rarely utilizes the performing potentials of an off-stage "real" physical space; instrumental simulations of spatial relationships as well as the other extra-musical representations, although quite common, were usually looked down upon. This disdain for the understanding of music as something that refers outside itself was the manifestation of philosophical and aesthetical trends of "absolute music," the nineteenth-century idea that became particularly important and controversial in twentieth-century aesthetics.[49]

What mattered in modern canonical works was the illusionary space "invented" by timbral combinations, harmonic progressions and other means of musical rhetoric: the imaginary soundscape independent from "the real space" of the concert hall. Although up to a certain point responsive to the acoustics of the space of the performing venue, these effects basically create an imaginary space of their own, similar to representations on the theater stage or in the painting. In other words, by the end of the seventeenth and beginning of the eighteenth centuries,

---

[47] *Man empfand die Welt zwar als poetisches Labyrinth Gottes, suchte aber nicht mehr nach dem Eingang oder auch nur nach dem Ausgang. Man blieb im Unentwirrbaren stecken.* Hocke, p. 14.

[48] In the third movement of Hector Berlioz's (1803–1869) *Fantastic Symphony* (1830), for instance, the onstage English horn and offstage oboe toss back and forth a melody, thus simulating shepherds' calls in the countryside. Gustav Mahler (1860–1911) also exploits similar effects in the final movement of his Second ("Resurrection") Symphony (1888–94) by placing an entire band of brass and percussion instruments behind the stage. The most memorable moment in this musical depiction of Judgment Day is when the offstage brass mimics "the great call" of heavenly fanfares while the onstage flutes imitate the bird song.

[49] This line of thought could be followed in nineteenth-century writings of E.T.A. Hoffmann and Eduard Hanslick, among many others, and its traces could be found in many twentieth-century discussions, including those by Carl Dahlhaus and Vladimir Jankélévitch.

the simulation of spatiality became incorporated and "framed" into musical works while its performance, in terms of visual perspective, became stage-centered. It would take a breakdown of the traditional modes of musical representation for this effect to reemerge in the genre of electro-acoustic music: that is, in the twentieth-century genres that include new technologies in sound (re)production, including "elektronische Musik," "musique concrète," electronic, tape, acousmatic, and computer music.

Electroacoustica and the Crisis of the Autonomy of the Performing Space

Hocke's description of the early modern self bears an uncanny resemblance to Max Ernst's auto-portrait that I discussed in my opening paragraph. Many similar twentieth-century "labyrinthine" self-visions by Man Ray, Salvador Dali, and Pablo Picasso come to mind as well. Notably, most of them were performed in the medium of photography that enabled new visual experiments. At this point, I will explain how twentieth-century music and its investment in new technologies reveal similar dilemmas of self-identification and sense of "the self in the world."

In the twentieth century, various experimentations with new technologies inside and outside of the studio brought about changes in musical perception. Electronically produced and reproduced sounds posed new questions. Is traditional representation, defined by physical limitations, important at all? How do electronic media change our understanding of a conventional division between referential (traditional or mimetic) and invented sounds? What is the meaning of the sound that moves provisionally from one speaker to another and surrounds the listener? Electro-acoustic genres epitomize the moment at which traditional representation becomes surpassed, not merely negated, because the choice of musical material completely changes the function of physical space. The sound material in electro-acoustic music is usually previously performed and recorded in the silence of a studio, before the official performance and separated from audience's gaze. In this context, performance based on the physicality of the human body – so crucial for modern performance – becomes less important. In electro-acoustic performances, mimetic or non-mimetic pre-recorded sounds, transmitted in various ways through space, change the basic expectations of the audience.

But if seventeenth-century "echo pieces" cover a wide range of mimetic possibilities – including natural acoustic phenomena and metaphors of interiority – electro-acoustic music "ignores" the relevance of realistic mimesis: the sound might be recognizable, but that is not the most relevant fact for its perception. The "storyline" is difficult to follow without a specific understanding of the sound material and the composer's intentions. I understand this modernist disassociation from the "common" understanding of a musical language as a pinnacle of "the narcissistic self" in music. The space of the performance hall, defined by a very specific position of speakers and electronically produced musical material, is an artificial space that does not have an outside reference; it is entirely the product of the composer's fantasy.

In the context of this discussion, more interesting than the nature of sound processing is the way electro-acoustic music becomes transmitted through space. Varèse's *Poeme électronique* (1958) and Xenakis's *Concert PH* (1958), disseminated through 425 loudspeakers at the Philips Pavilion of the Brussels Exposition (1958), or the permanent loudspeaker installations by Groupe de Musique Expérimentale de Bourges (*Gmebaphone*, 1973) and Groupe de Recherches Musicale in Paris (*Acousmonium*, 1974) testify to the experimental thread in European music that researches the nature of sound diffusion in a way that resembles early modern negotiations with performance.

As in echo performances, the sources of sound in electro-acoustic music – in this case loudspeakers – are placed at various distances from listeners in differing points of a performing hall to aurally simulate a sort of topographical relief. Speakers in differing positions transmit various types of sounds thus imitating the dissemination of sound in a "natural" environment. During performance, the person who takes care of the sound diffusion can also control and shape the creation of sound "relief." In such a performing situation, the listener is not "gazing" into the stage presentation of the performing music, but is in a middle of it.

But before examining the pieces in which musical material completely divorces itself from the centuries-long tradition of musical language through technological manipulation, I would like to examine a twentieth-century piece that exploits the notion of "spatial" music in a way that echoes my seventeenth-century examples, thus influencing and changing the listener's perception. The piece *Laborintus II* (1965) by Luciano Berio creates a compromise between the traditional musical language and a need for its reinvention.

Berio in *Laborintus II*, as in many of his other works (*Epifanie, Simfonia, Formazioni, Concerto II*), examines the role of space for the musical perception of the listener. In the introduction to the score Berio suggests: *"Laborintus II* may be presented as a theatrical event, a narrative, an allegory, a documentary, a pantomime etc. It may be performed in theatre, in concert, on television, on the radio, in the open air, etc".[50] Interestingly, the composer does not think that this piece should be exclusively performed in the physical space of the concert hall, since he has no objections to technologically transmitted musical performances. Technology is a primary influence for Berio, and his fondness for technologically modified sound shows in the fact that *Laborintus II* brings together acoustic instruments, electrically modified voices (all the vocal performers, including the singers, actors/*coro* and the speaker/*testo* should use microphones), electronic tape and loudspeakers. On the other hand, his concern about the use of microphones and the position of the loudspeakers shows his interest in the spatial effects of music. He leaves this decision open to the producer and the conductor, who have to make their choices depending on the venue where the piece is performed. In a

[50] Luciano Berio, *Laborintus II* (Milano: Universal edition, 1976).

stage-centered performance, the loudspeakers should be up front, transmitting the sound of a rather traditionally positioned stage.

Laborintus II represents a labyrinth of words and voices. Berio wrote it for French radio for the celebration of Dante's seven-hundredth birthday. He conveniently chose various texts – from the Bible to Dante's lyrics and contemporary poetry – in order to represent seven centuries of culture that embraced the ideas of Western humanism; it is a labyrinth of events, thoughts, and opinions that presents a short interpretation of modern Western history in words. The metaphor of the labyrinth could describe the relationship between vocal as well as instrumental parts in this piece. The labyrinthine effect, as in the case of simulated aural prosecution in the example by Schütz, turns every listener into a subject, the one who experiences the mish-mash of diverse lyrics and sounds that begin and stop almost at random. The role of the speaker (*testo*) very often, as in seventeenth-century cantatas and oratorios, assumes the role of the subject. However, in *Laborintus II*, the simulation of spatial relations becomes a crucial part of the composition: the voices are amplified differently; sometimes they sound as if coming from the distance and sometimes their loudness simulates spatial proximity. The speaker does have a significant role, and not rarely does the entire piece have a character of hallucination: the actors and singers together with the speaker create an imaginary soundscape – a narrative-musical labyrinth that tells the story of collective memory in poetry.

If *Laborintus II* shows Berio's interest in various possibilities of music transmission, the use of loudspeakers becomes crucial for the understanding of Stockhausen's "elektronische Musik." As in Berio's piece, the performance takes place in a physical space defined by the sound coming from loudspeakers. *Gesang Der Jünglinge* (1956) is composed for five groups of loudspeakers distributed in space around the listeners.[51] Stockhausen carefully planned the direction and movement of the sound in advance. After the world premiere, he realized that his plan to combine a 4-track tape recorder with a fifth channel performed on a mono-tape recorder (hanging from the ceiling of the performing hall) turned out to be difficult to realize, so he transformed the piece into a 4-track composition, which means that four loudspeakers are used for the performance: each loudspeaker transmits one track. The musical material, however, is almost completely non-referential; it is difficult to decipher its sources and ways of creation. Electronically produced sounds, a modified human voice, and a vague indication of instrument noises are put together in a seemingly non-coherent fragmentary whole: an auditory attack of unrecognizable musical materials sounds as if someone is very quickly changing radio stations. Stockhausen treats musical fragments like sound objects rather than parts of a temporal musical whole. In this case, it is futile to try to look for a point of reference in previous listening experiences or familiar mimetic

---

[51]   This again recalls early modern performing habits. Nino Pirrotta discusses "stereophonic effects" of Florentine *intermedi* with "dialogues between groups that were dispersed – on earth, in midair, or in apertures in the heavens." Pirrotta, p. 211.

representations of space. Because Stockhausen creates previously unheard sonic material, an immediate understanding of the music becomes impossible. A listener new to these sounds will need to reinvent a musical vocabulary for this listening experience.

Stockhausen claims that his main idea in *Gesang Der Jünglinge* was to unify vocal and electronically produced sounds to the point that it becomes difficult to make a distinction between the two. Indeed, sometimes the vocal praise of God that is taken from *The Song of the Youths in the Fiery Furnace* (the Third Book of Daniel) becomes easily recognizable, and, at other times, the electronically produced sounds seem overwhelmingly "synthetic." But there are also moments when it becomes difficult to decipher if the sound coming from loudspeakers is human or electronic manipulation. Stockhausen was not interested in the literary value of words, which is why he decided to use a more "universal" type of content in praising God: in the listening process, one does not have to focus on semantic meaning; the words are like a prayer whose sense resides in meditative repetition and not in intellectual contemplation. Admittedly, Stockhausen wanted to equalize the human and the artificial: he even influenced a young boy's performance by asking him to imitate the synthetic sounds he would previously record.[52] In this case, the human voice is intentionally subordinated to technology. The composer creates the illusion that voice and electronic sound belong to the same realm of human endeavor. By blurring the distinction between the two and playing a trick on his audience, he challenges their ability to differ between the natural and artificial. In appropriating this "acousmatic" philosophy ("what I hear is what I know"), Stockhausen wants his audience to accept the products of the new technology in the same way as they would accept a "traditional" notion of music: that is, the voice. In comparison, the role of the electronic tape in Berio's *Laborintus* seems oddly displaced because of its location within the context of the piece: the "tape-solo" of intentionally hyper-synthesized sounds takes place only at the very end of the composition; it is a strange interpolation of the technological body that reminds the listeners of what is to come after centuries of human-centered culture.

In this kind of treatment of the musical material, the definition of acousmatic music, the music that explores "sound in itself," becomes very helpful. "Akousmatikoi" or "those willing to hear," were Pythagoras's pupils who were required to listen to their teacher's speeches while he was speaking hidden behind the screen. This situation of "listening without seeing" was very often used in twentieth-century music in explaining various experiments with sounds produced by new technologies. From this point of view, "pure sound" should be appreciated for what it becomes at the moment of silent contemplation, without reference to its sources or ways of production. This "listening without seeing" becomes crucial for

---

[52] Karlheinz Stockhausen, *Elektronische Musik 1952–1960* (Kürten, Germany: Stockhausen, 1991), Compact disc.

the understanding of the musical material created by sound synthesis, so common in today's music production, but so new in the 1950s and '60s.

I don't believe, however, in the possibility of "innocent" hearing. Even when one does not see the source of sound while listening, there are other factors that shape perception, whether based on experience or imagination. On one hand, I find the ideals of the "acousmatic" approach to music experience relevant to a discussion of an important twentieth-century paradigm shift (the exploration of music as sound); and on another, they are the continuation of the nineteenth-century doctrine of absolute music.

The most interesting question is what happens to the perception of space and the human place within it in these kinds of performances. Very often in the literature on twentieth-century music, there is a significant distinction made between the conception of space in *musique concrète* and in "elektronische Musik." While *musique concrète* allows and even requires performers' interventions and control over the interaction with space at the time of the performance, electronic music is preconceived: every speaker transmits one channel creating the sound-wall carefully planned by the composer. But this distinction is not crucial for the listeners' perception. It could be explained as a distinction between improvised (and thus only somewhat open) and fixed composition.

What is more important, however, is that both types of music include the notion of physical space in the composing process. Hoping to start a musical revolution, Stockhausen, in *Gesang Der Jünglinge*, experimented with the use of loudspeakers for the first time in music history. With this experimentation, however, he had a particular goal in mind. In his own words: "By incorporating controlled positioning of the sound sources in space, it will have been possible for the first time to demonstrate aesthetically the universal application of my integral serial technique."[53] Stockhausen, then, wanted to use this new technology in order to "persuade" the audience of the universality of his new highly fixed and organized musical language. And by doing so, he projected his own subjectivity – his understanding of language and space – onto the audience. In Berio's piece, the situation is slightly different: *Laborintus* is open to interpretation; its musical material, both acoustic and electronic, is performed live, and it is quite possible to include new understandings of space that do not necessarily correspond with the composer's. In other words, by ignoring the autonomy of the performing stage and by including the totality of spatial perspective enabled by the loudspeakers as aural prostheses, both Stockhausen and Berio redefine musical structure. Berio's refusal of control over some performing choices, however, points towards the concept of the open work as defined by Eco while Stockhausen's, at every moment a precisely prescribed and controlled process of composition, displays a subjectivity that is still very much self-focused and controlling.

To go back to the introductory note on *opera aperta*: Umberto Eco was not particularly concerned with the notion of space and its influence on the art work.

---

[53]   Ibid.

As a semiotician, he was more fascinated by works that somehow subvert the order of the text. Thus, when saying that in twentieth-century literature "an ordered world based on universally acknowledged laws is being replaced by a world based on ambiguity, both in the negative sense that directional centers are missing and in a positive sense, because values and dogma are constantly being placed in question," Eco is obviously focused on the structural laws that govern the standard logic of story telling or music making. It is interesting, however, that he mostly focuses on composers who negotiate between the obsessive control over the material (integral serialism) and the possibility of performing freedom ruled by chance (aleatoric).[54]

While Eco's theory serves as one of my main theoretical leads, I wish to approach to the problem of openness from a different angle. As I have tried to demonstrate in this chapter, musical texts interest me as material proof of the ever-changing understanding of the world; as documents of the history of a certain phenomenon that reveal reasons for its emergence. My focus is on explaining, not exclusively the subversion of the laws of musical structure as the tokens of the crisis of modernity, but also on the development of the mindset and cultural conditions that made this crisis possible. Thus, unlike Eco, I don't want to equate pieces that allow the performer the freedom to choose the order of structural sections with pieces that more significantly involve the performer (or the audience) in the performing process. In the latter case, the illusion of an imagined stage-frame and the authority of the composer and the performer are questioned more radically.

In both cases, however, the traditional stage-oriented performance poses a significant problem. If the audience sits in the position in which their gaze is directed toward the stage, the effect electro-acoustic music aims at becomes significantly lessened. Therefore, the performance that employs loudspeakers demands a thorough redefinition of a concept of performing venue that dominated Western culture for a couple of centuries despite some attempts to "occupy" sight in performing situations by using other media (theater, ballet, film) to "fill-out" the stage-space. The other, more wide spread option in contemporary listening habits is to experience electroacoustica in the privacy of a personal space where sound dissemination through loudspeakers does not pose a significant problem, and certain popular genres of electronica that are more aimed at intellectual perception are usually consumed that way. In the context of public performance, however, it seems that popular electronic genres offer the most satisfying effects: a disc-jockey could be placed at any position of the performing venue; the audience's gaze becomes less relevant; the focus is on the dancing and personal physical

---

[54]   Eco focuses on Stockhausen's *Klavierstück XI*, Boulez's Third piano sonata, Berio's *Circles*, and Pousser's *Mobile*. All these pieces combine integral serialism with controlled aleatoric. In *Klavierstück XI* and Third piano sonata the performer(s) can choose the order of sections, in *Circles* – rhythm and pitch, and in *Mobile* the possible continuations of sections.

experience through bodily expression. In Egginton's terms, the focus shifts again from *theatricality* to *presence* in which audience members become more aware of the space and their own place in it. In this way, vernacular music genres manage to escape the awkwardness of perception that electroacoustica oftentimes causes even today when performed in traditional performing venues.

While in early modern pieces, the notion of the phenomenological, formal, or aesthetical whole posed significant questions and was negotiated in various ways, it seems that the electro-acoustical genre dismisses its importance: the logic of the exposition of sound material in electro-acoustic music is usually teleologically undefined, and it becomes rather difficult and less relevant to perceive beginnings and endings. On the other hand, this is not exclusively a feature of electro-acoustic music, but also of other genres of twentieth century modernism and avant-garde. I have chosen electroacoustica rather than some other genre because it more thoroughly questions our listening habits. The majority of modernist and avant-garde works are "trapped" in negotiating, either through confirmation or negation, the concept of the autonomy of the musical work. Electro-acoustic works overcome this dilemma, and deal with the more general phenomenological understanding of music. What is significant in electro-acoustic works is that the spatial qualities of music and sound in general become more significant than temporal ones. In this sense, they completely redefine our traditional notions of the musical work as described by Eco in my opening paragraph. The idea of the whole as a (teleo) logical temporal happening here becomes quite irrelevant: as in Baroque art when sculpture and painting questioned the very medium by using the logic of theater or narration, electro-acoustical music questions temporality as the most relevant phenomenon in the perception of music. If in the conventional sense the musical piece should be a temporal whole with a logical beginning, development, and conclusion, electroacoustica questions this notion and "frosts" the temporality of music into the spatiality of sound installation. In comparison with seventeenth-century pieces, in which spatiality only managed to influence the affective language, in twentieth century electro-acoustic pieces, spatiality ruled out temporality as the most relevant phenomenological feature of sound.

Berio's piece marks out the furthest point in music history to which I will refer in this study. It epitomizes the moment in which traditional representation becomes surpassed, not only negated. In subsequent chapters, I will mostly refer to the pieces that are in between the negation and the reconstitution of language. Stockhausen's and Berio's works, though, enable me to describe the break first, then go back and explain what led up to it. In the next chapter, I will explain how the notion of a "theatrical space" changed the language and dramaturgy of musical composition; I will show how musical structures had been established, and how they disintegrated in the twentieth century. I will discuss works in which the stage becomes conquered; it becomes a venue for the display of modern subjectivity in church, court, or theater. Even when not staged, music was guided by principles of oratory as primarily an acted performance. This musical-theatrical display of selfhood, formed under the influence of classical oratory, had a predicable dramaturgy that included closure as one of the obligatory elements. But, just as composers explored the role and limits of space in early modern music, they also questioned this newly conquered musical dictionary and modes of representation.

Chapter 2
The Unutterable Silence:
O Word, Thou Word that I Lack

1910 – The Beginning of the End

The most problematic issue with the analogy between historical periods that I propose is their transitional character. The ends of the sixteenth and, especially, the seventeenth centuries are as heterogeneous culturally as the first half of the twentieth century is, as is obvious in art production. It may be rather difficult to discuss late modernity and not to begin, speaking in stylistic terms again, with expressionism, which opened the "end" of the modern era. Thomas Harrison sees this early twentieth-century style as a phenomenon which had occurred in various forms and in various geographic areas.[1] He chooses the events that took place in the year 1910 as the key historical reference from which to comment on the conclusion of one period in modern Western history and the beginning of another one. He claims that in the seven years to either side of "nineteen ten" some of the most startling changes in modern history happened, including drastic reshufflings of nations, economies, societies, and psyches, as well as artistic, scientific, and political revolutions.[2] Among the most poignant contemporary descriptions of this historical moment as seen by contemporaries comes one from an American, Henry Adams, whose words Harrison uses to demonstrate the growing nihilism in European culture, words that uncannily resemble pessimistic descriptions of Baroque Europe by José Antonio Maravall:

> Every reader of the French and German newspapers knows that not a day passes without producing some uneasy discussion of supposed social decrepitude; falling off of the birthrate; – decline of rural population, – lowering of army standards; – multiplication of suicides; – increase of insanity or idiocy; – of cancer; – of tuberculosis; – signs of nervous exhaustion, – of enfeebled vitality, – 'habits' of alcoholism and drugs, – failure of eyesight in the young, – and so on, without end.[3]

---

[1]   Thomas Harrison, *1910: The Emancipation of Dissonance* (Berkeley: University of California Press, 1996).

[2]   Ibid., p. 9.

[3]   Ibid., p. 7.

Expressionism is conventionally related to Dresden and Munich, but in music, the most relevant center for the years preceding World War I is surely Vienna, and the composers whose works I take into consideration (Strauss, Schoenberg, Berg) all had one significant expressionist phase that stylistically and spiritually corresponded with the art of *Die Brücke* or *Der Blau Reiter*. In the second chapter, I will explain how the cuts intentionally inflicted on musical wholes in works of musical expressionism reflect the beginning of the end about which Harrison writes.

Lacking the Words, Lacking the Other

Ich suchte … utters the heroine in her final words of Schoenberg's *Erwartung* (1909). Throughout the monodrama, she is looking for something, or someone, her other, supposedly her lover whom she never manages to reach. Far more ominous than the mythical Narcissus, she is a character trapped in the darkness of her subconscious. There is no naïveté in her illusion: not seeing beauty in herself or in the other, she is just wandering in the dark, hopelessly looking for something palpable, something that will give her security. Instead, she only manages to stumble upon the dead body of her lover. A nightmarish psychological state, in Adorno's words "the eternity of the second in four hundred bars," is simulated with tonally disoriented, fragmented expressionistic phrasing that originates from the monodrama's narrative content.

The first scene already displays the key "ingredients" of an expressionistic poetics: the moon; an unfamiliar dark wood; a path, here only vaguely suggested but uncovered again and again with great difficulty throughout the inner journey that the woman hesitantly undertakes, the journey into the woods of her subconscious for the loved one "buried" in the memory of her past.

Entering the unknown sharpens the senses: she can't see the path, but she sees the trees gleam; she feels the warmth of the night and oppressive air and – most important – fear before this internal adventure. The first tone is G♯ in a quite disoriented tonal environment that most closely resembles D. This first tone (which is going to be the last too) is all telling, translating the dreadfulness and unsteadiness of the narrative into the tonal language itself. It is not only the G♯ that creates this uneasiness in the instrumental beginning. The continuing motives are short, spread out unevenly throughout the orchestra, clumsy in their discontinuous dissonant jumps: there's a bassoon first, and then the rest of the woodwinds with celesta, a more audible oboe solo, and then just a shiver in the strings and harp.

This ostensible chaos, however, is very well thought through and organized. Upon closer examination, we find that any reminiscences of tonality are purposefully and strategically avoided. The first two beats expose almost all the tones of a chromatic scale, layered in perfect and augmented fourths (ten tones actually, in the following order – G, D, G♯, G♭, C, F, B, E, B♭, E♭). The mentioned first tone, the ominous G♯ as an augmented fourth to D, first announces

Schoenberg's way out of the tonal system. Nothing confirms better the composer's intention than the sudden occurrence of a major third (the two left-out tones from the above mentioned series – A/C♯). In this context, the consonance of the third sounds out of place, but as is everything in *Erwartung*, it is dramatically justified: by supporting the oboe solo – something that finally resembles a real melody and announces the vocal part, the major third gives a glimpse of a supposed sanity, or the remembrance of one. That this is only an illusion is clear immediately after the oboe melody does not develop in an expected way; it does not follow tonal logic. Instead, it deviates (C♯, B, A♯ instead of C♯, B, A), only to disperse itself in dissonant jumps (in fourths, of course).

The voice part, in accordance with tradition, imitates the solo from the instrumental introduction but in a more elaborated version. Only now, with the entry of narrative content, it becomes clear where all the anxiety comes from. The woman hesitates to enter the forest (*Go in there?/Hier hinein?*) and then explains why (*I can't see the path/ Man sieht den Weg nicht*). The explanation results in a sudden ascending jump of the minor seventh, expressing her fear of the unknown with the ominous concluding G♯. And her emotional and mental sensitivity reflects itself not only through her narrated awareness of the changing environment (*How silvery the tree trunks gleam ... like birches!/ Wie silbern die Stämme schimmern ... wie Birken*) but also through another tessitura change and a tonally and rhythmically nervous descending part.

Erwartung is a description of a phantasm, a combination of psychological apparition and emotional hallucination. The narration that shivers between constant questioning and negation never brings the affirmation of the woman's actual existence.[4] As the first scene whose introductory measures I described above unfolds, the narration of the main character encompasses a wide array of non-affirmative rhetoric gestures. The woman questions herself (*Go in there? Aren't you going to look for him? Can it see in there?/Hier hinein? Willst ihn nich suchen? Sieht der hinein?*); she comments in negation (*I can't see. Don't speak. Die here./Man sieht ... nicht ... Nicht sprechen ... So stirb doch hier ...*); or she speaks in foreboding phrases (*oppressive air, motionless storm, awfully quiet and empty, menacing silence, aghast moon/ Schwere Luft ... Ein Sturm der steht ... Grauenvoll ruhig und leer ... Wie drohend die Stille ist ... Der Mond ist Entsetzen*). Today we know that Schoenberg had significant input into Marie Pappenheim's libretto writing, which allows us to say a great deal about his artistic intentions in creating *Erwartung*. A non-confirmative rhetoric, a nihilistic narration of some

---

[4] I am aware of the interpretations of *Erwartung* in the light of psychoanalysis and especially in the context of Freudian case-studies of the female psyche. But, as I explained earlier, my focus is on the phenomenological conditions that precede the internal psychological conditions, on the body as the exterior object that is taking part in the general exchange of rhetorical signs. Even if I do look into the causes for a specific inner emotional and psychological state, the direction is always from outside to inside, from culture as the trigger of change to the subject as a receiver of this cultural influence.

sort, is Schoenberg's main preoccupation on both levels of storytelling, on the narrative and the musical unfolding.

The rhetoric of *Erwartung* does not include exclusively negative elements. There is a realistic confirmative narrational thread in the woman's constant observations about her surroundings. First, when talking about the outer world, she notices the moon and the night. The night as her subconscious and the moon, an ambiguous signifier of both her hopes and fears, stand as the central, exterior signifiers of the woman's innerness.[5] In addition, while sensual things still seem perceptible to her, actual events and people are only remembrances in her memory. Schoenberg not only translates this narrative outburst of a complex interior state into music, but he also builds up the tension, enhancing the sense that every description of exteriority has as its purpose only to reflect the interiority of the subject. He depicts the warmth of the night with tam-tam and violin flageolet, personifies hope with the clear (*deutlich*) sound of celesta and harp, and presents the cricket song in the "romantic" strings.

While the second scene repeats the rhetoric strategies of the first one, the third scene brings about a dramatic and musical development: the apparitions are more vivid and more complex (*Something black dancing there ... hundred hands ... it's the shadow ... like your shadow on the white walls/ Dort tanzt etwas Schwarzes ... hundert Hände ... es ist der Schatten ... wie dein Schatten auf die weissen Wände fällt ...*) foreshadowing the complexity of the final scene, which brings about the climax of the woman's confrontation with her suppressed fears of abandonment and betrayal. This scene culminates with her cry for help (*Hilfe!*) as the statement that probably sounds as the most truthful statement in *Erwartung*. Her final words (*I was looking ...*), however, might as well be the opening ones. It is as if nothing had happened by the end of this piece, too short for the operatic genre but nonetheless nearly unbearably extensive, given its obsessive affective reiteration.

The final and the introductory tones of *Erwartung* are the same (G♯) so there is a certain conclusion to this piece, in a quite traditional manner. But in the absence of a tonal center, that conclusiveness is not something perceivable, something that gives a real sense of the whole. If we consider that the modern musical whole is basically defined by its tonal logic, then Schoenberg's intention becomes quite clear: this is an antithesis to the traditional notion of the whole – its negative, ironical counterpart. Schoenberg, however, as Adorno claimed, despite his destructive tendency, always had a totality in view: "For its sake he left to one side everything that merely laid claim to totality, instead of creating one."[6]

Schoenberg's microscopic exploration of one affect – dreadful anticipation – epitomizes the early twentieth-century sense of nihilism. The ultimate source

---

[5]   This expressionistic poetics repeats again in the grotesque representation of subjectivity in *Pierrot Lunaire* (1912). The extreme moods change from *Drunk with moonlight* (first song) to *The sick moon* (seventh song).

[6]   Theodor W. Adorno, *Quasi una Fantasia: Essays of Modern Music*, trans. Rodney Livingstone (London, New York: Verso, 1992), p. 233.

of fear is to be locked in oneself, without the ability to reach the other, actually to be able only to discover the fact of the other's non-existence. For the feeling of being alone and tangled in *Erwartung* reflects an alienation that entirely excludes otherness.

The concepts of music as an expressive "language," on the one hand, and as an abstract system of tonal organization, on the other, come together and work for/against each other in Schoenberg expressionist phase: while *Erwartung* still offers the traces of tonality and expressive rhetoric, it simultaneously undoes them. In this sense, the way Schoenberg negotiates between traditional modes of musical representation and the formation of a new system of musical expression is strikingly similar to experiments in visual arts of the same period, most notably Vasily Kandinsky's negotiations between figuration and abstraction. Thomas Harrison elaborates on this transitory phase between representation and abstraction in Kandinsky's work:

> Kandinsky's paintings of these years contain both types of elements: dissolving forms of the material world – mountain peaks, churches, horses, boats, and riders – as well as abstract patterns. Works such as *Untitled (First Abstract Watercolor)* (dated 1910, but more likely from 1913) and *Improvisation XI* (1910) present the derealization of the physical world as an impetus for new and alternative constructions.[7]

Harrison's words on Kandinsky very much correspond with Adorno's conclusion about Schoenberg's relationship toward tradition: "Schoenberg's works melted down all the formal categories from which traditional music has hoped to create a self-contained, rounded totality that denied anything outside of its cosmos."[8]

But at the time of the formation of these categories in early modernity, there was significant experimentation with how should they appear. In the rise of modernity, the change in the status of music enabled the development of its representational powers and the formation of a recognizable musical language through which we comprehend the meaning of in canonical works. In the mid-sixteenth century, the increased interest in the expressiveness of the musical language as opposed to its mathematical bases led to the development of musical rhetoric. Instead of embodying an ethical ideal or resembling the harmony of the spheres, music for the first time discovered the potential of its own language. In the world of *natural magic*, to use Gary Tomlinson's term, or I would add, in a premodern world, the resemblance of the tones and intervals to the harmony of the spheres, colors, precious stones, or horoscope signs was conveniently symbolized by numbers and

---

[7] Harrison, p. 58.
[8] Adorno, p. 233.

proportions.[9] The *loss of magic*, on the other hand, together with the discovery of human creative potential, posed new challenges and questions.[10] What is musical representation? Can music function as a narrative? What is the role of space in musical performance? How do we capture spontaneous improvisation? In the sixteenth century, music definitely became a creative expressive medium, shifting from the *quadrivium* (liberal arts that also included arithmetic, geometry, and astronomy) to the *trivium* (with grammar, rhetoric, and logic). But this division between the understanding of music as a mathematical discipline and music as rhetorical performance has never been completely overcome; it is still alive even today, repeated in conflicts between interpretations of music as the reflection of divine and cosmic relations versus music as language, and between music as nature versus music as artifice. This division becomes central to Schoenberg's revolutionary replacement of musical expressivity with logical systematic order – a change that concludes the centuries-long role of music as an expressive medium.

Sixteenth-century musical experiments were inspired in part by interest in classical Greek tragedy as a perfect artistic form in which poetry holds superiority over music. Attempts at recreating the ancient ideal resulted in an understanding that music should primarily serve to underline the meaning of words. In his collection of songs for one voice, *Le Nuove Musiche*, which is conventionally taken as the turning point in the development of monody, Giulio Caccini refers to Plato and other philosophers who thought that speech is most important for music "with the aim that it enters into the minds of men and makes those wonderful effects admired by the great writers." Caccini critiques counterpoint and the *passagi* that disable the understanding of the words. He composed the songs for one voice because they have "more power and delight and move one" more than several voices together.[11]

Despite the fact that the shift from polyphony to monody significantly facilitated the understanding of musical affectations, composers tried to look for new ways

---

[9]   The Renaissance music as magical practice is explored in Gary Tomlinson. *Music in Renaissance Magic: Toward a Historiography of Others* (Chicago and London: University of Chicago Press, 1993).

[10]   The "loss of magic" that Tomlinson discusses in relation to the status of music is a constant topic in the history of ideas. The oldest and the most popular is Max Weber's theory of "disenchantment," which is more focused on social issues and the development of capitalism. But the essence is the same: disenchantment as well as the loss of magic denotes the lack of the belief in a causally connected universe, in which all elements somehow resemble and reflect each others' existences. From this perspective, music loses its ability to reflect higher natural order as it acquires rhetorical power.

[11]   Giulio Caccini, *Le Nuove Musiche*, introduction to *Recent Researches in the Music of the Baroque Era*, vol. 9, ed. H. Wiley Hitchcock, (Madison: A-R Editons, Inc., 1970), p. 44.

of expression by using both types of textures, especially in madrigals.[12] Nowhere is this experimental thread more apparent than in the madrigals of Gesualdo da Venosa (1561–1613). The ways he violated the rules of counterpoint in his late output can only be justified as stemming from his general discontent with musical language. And, as in Schoenberg's work, Gesualdo's violation of the musical language, springs from the tormented innerness expressed in the text: *I shall die miserable, in my suffering/ and the one who could give me life/ alas, kills me and is unwilling to give me aid!/ O painful fate/ The one who could give me life, gives me death! (Moro, lasso, al mio duolo/ E chi mi può dar vita/ Ahi, che m'ancide e non vuol darmi aita!/ O dolorosa sorte/ Chi dar vita mi può, ahi mi dà morte!).* It is unknown who wrote the lyrics, possibly Gesualdo himself. Whatever the case, the obsession with death and suffering is quite poignant. Here, there is no hope on the horizon, only the certainty of an end. And the music could be hardly understood by using any familiar approach: open chromaticism in all voices and wrongly conducted imitations seem like a disturbing caricature of what a madrigal should be. With a suspicious eagerness that is too often dismissed as a plain neurosis, he travesties the common conventions of the genre.[13] His experiments with dissonance seemed as transgressive to his contemporaries.

There are too many speculations about Gesualdo's life and work. Of course, his social status as the prince of Venosa, his financial and artistic independence, enabled him "the luxury of solipsism,"[14] that would later on become a dream of every romantic artist. Too often Gesualdo is hailed as some kind of pre-expressonist, a predecessor to twentieth-century dissonance. Speaking in terms of musical technique, however, this is not really accurate. For Gesualdo extends the limits of modality, not tonality, producing dissonances as a product of clash

---

[12] Nino Pirrotta reminds us that the idea of reviving classical drama permeated all musical genres, including madrigals. He claims that "the constant preoccupation with madrigals, both in *Dialogo* and in (Vicenzo) Galilei's other writings, shows that the (Florentine) Camerata looked upon them as the highest and most complete form of expression in the music – at any rate the secular music – of their day; they criticized madrigals not because they wanted to do away with them but because they wanted to reform them and give them new life." Nino Pirrotta, "Temperaments and Tendencies in the Florentine Camerata," *Music and Culture in Italy from the Middle Ages to the Baroque* (Cambridge, Massachusetts, and London, England: Harvard University Press, 1984), p. 220.

[13] Susan McClary claims that "Gesualdo appears to identify alternations of speed – between exaggeratedly slow-motion harmonic changes and quicksilver motivic exchange – as fundamental elements of interiority," similar to some sort of bipolar psychological disturbances. McClary also claims, however, that "a twentieth-century doctor might have prescribed lithium for the bipolar disturbances traced in these madrigals – and we would have missed out on these attempts at simulating radical mood swings through the cultural medium of sixteenth-century modality." Susan McClary, *Modal Subjectivities: Self-Fashioning in the Italian Madrigal* (Berkeley: University of California Press, 2004), p. 149.

[14] Ibid., p. 146.

of horizontally independent counterpoint parts, not as a way of sabotaging the vertical sonority of the chord. This does not, however, change the fact that his dissonances communicate (and cause) emotional strain, at time significantly less understandable and more difficult to comprehend than twentieth-century ones. And from this perspective, he is some kind of long forgotten predecessor to the emotional intensity of expressionists.

I mentioned Gesualdo, the most extreme experimenter of his time, because he embodies two important elements of a rising modern subjectivity: the sense of creative potential and the difficulties to negotiate its limits. He is among the first musical figures to justify Hauser's words: "Renaissance individualism reached its culmination in the concept of the genius, which implied the possibility of conflict between the creative personality and rules, teaching and tradition, and made the artist more important than his work."[15] On the level of musical language, Gesualdo's musical distortions communicate existential angst similar to that in Schoenberg's piece: the impossibility of continuation and a desire to leave because there is no one to stay for; the sense of loneliness and alienation that, as I want to show, permeates not only secular but sacred genres as well.

The Secular Sacred: The Origins of Modern Anguish

I would like to take a look at some early modern predecessors of anomic modernist subjectivity as displayed in *Ewartung*, addressing the historical and cultural trajectory that led from the early modern cognition of the impossibility of reaching either the other or God to the nihilism of expressionism's unreachable otherness. As I mentioned above, I will mainly look at pieces that belong to the genre of sacred music because, in the historical and cultural contextualization of my discussion, religion – Catholicism and, up to a certain point when discussing confluences, Protestantism – greatly shaped the formation of modern identity. This thesis is convenient for my purposes because a majority of the musical genres that define the canonical repertoire originated from performing practices related to the church. Their profile changed from sacred to secular with general political and social changes in European society. With the decline of court and church as the main institutional supporters of musical activities, musical genres "migrated" to the public performing stage, reflecting the taste of the bourgeois audience. Most of them (sonata, concerto, symphony) adjusted to the requirements of the new audience, and even the ones that were closely tied to church rituals (mass, motet, psalm, oratorio) went though significant transformations, oftentimes being performed in the concert hall.[16]

---

[15] Arnold Hauser, *Mannerism: The Crisis of the Renaissance and the Origin of Modern Art*, trans. Eric Mosbacher (Cambridge: Harvard University Press, 1986), p. 33.

[16] The influence, again, goes in both directions. In the first place, the sacred music gets performed in the concert hall, and secondly, it became significantly influenced by secular

The discussion of "secularization theory" has been constantly reopened in the last few decades. In the social sciences and humanities, theorists started to question the oftentimes neglected influence of religion on the modern period of European history, in which the secular state presumably bases its legitimacy on separation from the church. To answer the dilemmas posed by secularization theory may seem out of place in this discussion. There is a need, however, to recognize the importance of religious influence, which has been often neglected not only in the understanding of sociological and political questions in the functioning of the institution of state, but also in wider social and cultural contexts, and more specifically in discussions of art. Musicology is only one of the disciplines born out of this tension between the secular and sacred.

In sociology, there is a very particular set of texts that problematize the pros and cons of the theory of secularization.[17] I am not as interested, however, in this particular discussion as much as I want to point out a general trend of separation of sacred and secular in various intellectual involvements with modern Western art and culture in the post-Enlightenment historiography. In this context, early modern subjectivity is rarely seen as the place of their confluence, but more commonly as the place of their separation.

In other words, too often the notion of the modern is characterized exclusively with its secular characteristics. A short aside into the visual arts can also reemphasize the relationship between the secular and sacred in early modern art. The most daring changes in visual artistic expression are also related to sacred places and spaces. The first example that comes to mind, the one preserved at the very heart of institutionalized Catholicism, Michelangelo's *Last Judgment*, shows in one significant segment the dread and despair of the eternally damned. Most memorable is one particular figure that shivers between heaven and hell: embraced by a demon – with his hand partly covering his face and with an uncovered eye filled with horror – he is depicted in the terrifying moment of recognizing his probable destiny. There is something uncanny about this figure, however, a kind of representational quality that goes beyond the dilemma of the Final Call. It seems as if this figure has a problem of his own, a problem of being caught in between, in the moment of not-knowing. The glory of the saved and the horror of the failed both look almost peaceful in comparison to this man's inner state. There is a certain empathy in this representation, a desire to show the horror of a moment in which one does not know what is ahead at the instant when there is no turning back – a

---

elements. Recall Mozart's masses, for example, in which certain soloist sections could be easily placed in one of his operas.

[17] For two texts that stand in opposition in regard to the importance of secularization as a consistent theory, see Jeffrey K. Hadden, "Toward Desacralizing Secularization Theory," *Social Forces*, vol. 65, no.3 (Mar., 1987): pp. 587–611; and Olivier Tschannen, "The Secularization Paradigm: A Systematization," *Journal of the Scientific Study of Religion*, vol. 30, no. 4 (Dec., 1991): pp. 395–415.

universal human feeling that could be related to inner turbulence caused by any number of external factors.[18]

Thinking about modern subjectivity in terms of religious identity goes against the long-lasting liberal influence on theory that traditionally celebrates the early modern recognition of human empowerment, emphasizing the "victories" of secularism in the Renaissance and in the Enlightenment. In art history, Arnold Hauser was among the first ones to dispute the theory of secularization, which since has been repeatedly challenged. Hauser "blames" Jules Michelet and Jacob Burckhardt for spreading this misconception of the Renaissance as exclusively the moment of the "discovery of man."[19] According to him, this widely spread misconception is a repercussion of the Enlightenment project and its ideological struggles. For liberal thinkers, every encounter with clericalism was seen as being dangerous for their intellectual goals. Although I agree with Hauser, I also understand that the idea of self-governance born out from the Enlightenment had to clash with the Christian morality of obedience. It is utterly another matter, however, to finally fully recognize that before this crisis of Christian authority started to develop in the late seventeenth and early eighteenth centuries, religion and morality were closely tied: almost every intellectual conflict had to do with the ideology of either the Reformation or the Counter-Reformation.[20]

From this perspective, early modern art is closely related to the campaign of propagating Catholic Church – the product of a devotional project crucial to the Counter-Reformation. Like the iconographical accounts of ecstatic spiritual

---

[18]   It is well-known that Michelangelo had a difficult and unpredictable relationship with the Medici Pope as well as long-lasting conflicting emotions towards the house of Medici. He was far from being satisfied in conducting this ambitious enterprise in the Sistine Chapel and very skeptical about its termination. It is easy to assume that the torn and tormented human figure is how Michelangelo sees himself because he did not feel in peace with his everyday life, let alone with his eternal prospects.

[19]   Hauser, *Mannerism*. Hauser's thesis is that secularization happened much earlier: the twelfth century saw many more drastic changes in economy, education, and urban organization.

[20]   To understand the most important shift in mentality of seventeenth-century Italian regions that are crucial for dealing with musical modernity means to understand the transformation of religion in the post-Reformation period. The Reformation movement – the "Copernican revolution of religion" – left permanent marks on the Catholic Church, which desperately wanted to revive its power. Its reaction had such a profound impact on all of Europe that, in fact, it seems impossible to discuss the culture of any European region without looking into the Counter-Reformation project. No matter how much humanist writers wanted to celebrate the first empirical scientists as the ones who brought light to European culture after the period of the dark Middle Ages, the transition to modernity was less secular in nature than is conventionally claimed. It is not the development of science alone that so radically changes the Western worldview: after all, Giordano Bruno was condemned more on the grounds of his belief in magic than because of his Copernican ideas.

experiences, art reinforces the mission of Catholic renewal. It would be wrong to say that this mission somehow diminishes the modern project. On the contrary, the subjective exploration of the world continued in part through representations of personal encounters with the divine. That is not to say there is something inherently subversive in them, or that they somehow bring about a secular agenda, but rather that there is no paradox in the formation of the self through religious fervor. These effects were allowed as the part of a larger project of the Counter-Reformation. Moreover, the church was ready to employ them as much as it did precisely because it wanted to find ways to renew its power over the Catholic community. In response to the threat of Protestant individuality, Catholics had to keep up with the trends of rising modernity. Rhetorical mastery was widely accepted by the Catholic clergy, guided by the Jesuits. Music rhetoricians followed the preaching technique that "simply molded the old message reaffirmed by the Council of Trent (1545–1563) to fit into forms provided by the world in which they themselves were immersed."[21]

The confluence of sacred and secular elements in this context is quite complex. Although the Council had posed very strict rules about church music composition (favoring Latin texts, Gregorian chant, clear polyphonic texture, and non-secular elements), the events that took place in the process of the Counter-Reformation shaped music somewhat differently, making it into a vehicle for the display of social and political power. In the previous chapter, in which I discussed the problem of space in the stage representations of the self, I commented on displays of social power; at this point I should stress the fact that the experiments with polychoralism that took place in Venetian and Roman churches were, in the first place, instruments of political promotion for the Counter-Reformation. Grandiose musical spectacles achieved by the use of multiple choirs placed on opposite sides of church galleries, with a great number of performers and the sonic "tricks" of dialoguing and echoing, created a rich sonority that is quite easy to compare with the exhibition of power in the secular performances of the Medici court.[22] The performed psalms, masses, and motets demonstrated the

---

[21] Rosario Villari, (ed.), *Baroque Personae*, trans. Lydia G. Cochrane (Chicago: University of Chicago Press, 1995), p. 131.

[22] In Rome, the secular and sacred meet in a real physical space: the Roman Piazza Navona served as the "theatre of the world" for the display of power of the Pope and his Pamphili family in the midst of the Counter-Reformation renewal. The message contained in the central position of Bernini's *Fountain of the Four Rivers* (*Fontana dei Quattro Fiumi*, 1651) at the Piazza is quite transparent: the power of the Catholic Church and its highest representatives extends to where the Danube, Ganges, Nile, and Rio della Plata reach. Moreover, the original arrangement of the Piazza should have included the Curia with its juridical and administrative palaces that today belong to Vatican. I gained this knowledge at the exhibition *Roma Baroca: Bernini, Borromini, Pietro da Cortona*, held from June 16 until October 29, 2006, in the *Castel Sant'Angelo* in Rome.

splendor of sacred spaces in the same way *intermedi* manifested the domination over the secular field of rule.[23]

In addition, the early modern rediscovery of rhetoric, especially in the writings of Quintilian and Cicero, greatly influenced the shaping of the modern musical language. Musical practice, however, had moved in a direction guided by the principles of rhetoric long before any consistent theory of musical figures or affects came into existence. As early as in the works of Josquin, affections inspired by traditional rhetoric permeated composing practice. And they stayed, in various forms, as part of modern musical language that would eventually lead toward Schoenberg and his denunciation of its foundation. Although the rulings of the Council were quite clear on matters of the secularization of church music, the development of musical rhetoric affected sacred genres as well. The affective musical language and nuances in text interpretation opened new ways to display religious devotion. From this perspective, the church was the place in which some of the most daring musical experiments took place, brought upon by social and cultural changes of the both religious renewal and developing individualism.

In the motet *O Vos Omnes* (1621) by Alessandro Grandi (*c*.1586–1630), for example, the "speaking" subject bewails the state of his people and his own destiny:

> O, all you who pass by the way,
> behold and see
> if there is any sorrow like my sorrow.
> Heavens be amazed at this,
> and their gates forcibly forsaken.
> Hear, o Heavens, and give ear, O earth,
> and be amazed:
> I have nurtured sons,
> but they have scorned me;
> I fed them with manna in the desert,
> but they have given me gall to eat;
> I gave them the waters of salvation,
> but they have given me vinegar to drink.
> Behold therefore and see
> if there is any sorrow like my sorrow.
> Hear, o Heavens, and give ear, O earth,
> and be amazed:

---

[23]   Andrea and Giovanni Gabrieli were famous Venetian representatives of this style. In Giovanni Gabrieli's (*c*.1555–1612) motet *In Ecclesiis* (publ. 1615), for example, a significant number of performers (the brass, strings, soloists, choir *a 15*, and organ) create a majestic sonority. There is no style or manner of composition of the time left out from this motet, and the interchange of various meters, textures, and bold modal changes are present as yet another token of social and political potency "translated" into music.

I have nurtured sons,
but they have scorned me;
I opened up the sea for them,
and they with the spear have opened my side;
for their sake I smote Egypt with the scourge
and they have given me up to the scourge.
Behold therefore and see
if there is any sorrow like my sorrow.[24]

These verses are culled from various sources – *Lamentations*, *Jeremiah*, and the *Psalms* – creating a thematically coherent whole that reveals more than just a freestyle approach to biblical texts: Grandi intentionally chose very particular types of verse from different but related sources in order to give the best musical representation of one particular emotion – sorrow. Musically, Grandi depicts this emotion in a succession of three types of material: an instrumental *sinfonia*, a free recitative, and a refrain. The most interesting section is the refrain, which adopts chromatic elements from the introductory instrumental *sinfonia*, but also further develops or, better said, *complicates* the chromatic progression. In the refrain (which, as we will see, not incidentally also closes the piece), there is an intentional sense of a tonal/modal disorientation that questions the logic of teleological musical development. The words of the refrain *behold and see if there is any sorrow like my sorrow*, become the narrative trigger for the musical dramaturgy of a warped vocal breakdown: the vertigo of shifting cadences so completely disorients the listener that the "proper" cadence at the very end sounds like the wrong tonal destination. More specifically, Grandi decides to repeat this syntagm three times as a chromatic descending phrase, each time on a different cadential point: the first time in D, then in G, and finally in the home key of C. By the end of the refrain, after the cadential "swirl," the home key becomes almost unrecognizable as such. The effect is not weakened by the repetitive structure of the entire motet: in the final repetition of the refrain – that is, in the conclusion to the piece – confusion over the key toward which the piece is supposedly "striving" leaves an entirely unhoped-for musical resolution. But the place of conclusion seems unrecognizable.

---

[24] *O vos omnes qui transitis per viam,/ attendite et videte/ si est dolor similis dolori meo./ Obstupescite caeli super hoc/ et porte ejus desolamini vehementer./ Audite caeli et aulibus percipe terra/ et obstupescite super hoc:/ filios enutrivi;/ ipsi autem spreverunt me/ et pavi eos manna per desertum;/ ipsi autem dederunt in escam meam fel,/ et aqua salutari potavi eos;/ ipsi autem in siti mea potaverunt me aceto./ Attendite ergo et videte/ si est dolor similis dolori meo./ Audite caeli et aulibus percipe terra/ et obstupescite super hoc:/ filios exaltavi;/ ipsi autem spreverunt me,/ ego ante eos aperuit mare;/ et ipsi lancea aperuerunt latus meum;/ ego propter eos flagellavi Aegyptum;/ et ipsi me flagellatum tradiderunt./ Attendite ergo et videte/ si est dolor similis dolori meo.*

This kind of musical experimentation is closely related to freedom in the use of sacred texts, which was typical for the genre of motet. Jerome Roche explains the flexibility of this genre, and conveniently in the context of this discussion, he uses the same example by Grandi in order to do so. Roche elaborates:

> (*O Vos Omnes*) … opens with the famous words from the *Lamentations* that begin the eponymous Tenebrae responsory and the section "attendite et videte si est dolor similis dolori meo" provides a striking chromatic refrain related musically to a chromatic string *sinfonia*. These refrain elements set off a series of verses freely paraphrased from the Good Friday Improperia, set to the most simple recitative-like music. One can imagine such a work being sung during the Veneration of the Cross on Good Friday, while the official texts of the Improperia prescribed to be sung during this act were quietly recited by the clergy. This is entirely in line with the practice of substituting Mass Propers or Office antiphons, common at the time, and illustrates why the motet should be regarded as a "paraliturgical" genre.[25]

The definition of the motet as a paraliturgical genre is very significant in discussing its musical characteristics. Because of its free style text treatment, it became the most convenient genre of sacred music in which early modern experiments with the potentials of musical rhetoric could take place. Freedom with regard to text choices opened the possibilities of experimenting with the *stile rappresentativo* and popular monody texture in a genre related to church performance. Roche explains its adaptability as some kind of fashion that resulted from performing practices: "many non-liturgical motet texts that Monteverdi and Grandi set, often for solo voice, were as likely to have been sung in aristocratic circles as in church: the indication *per cantar et sonar col chitarrone* on the title pages of some of Grandi's *motetti con sinfonie* suggests as much."[26]

I don't want to claim that Grandi's motet is a kind of seventeenth-century *Erwartung*. Its display of disoriented innerness, however, certainly has something in common with Schoenberg's monodrama. The suddenness and boldness of the chromatic movement through differing tonal centers creates an effect of emotional strain that has resembles the expressionistic negation of teleological progression. As a matter of fact, Grandi in this piece uses this figure that will become a typical way of signifying sorrow in subsequent European art music.[27] Recall that

---

[25] Jerome Roche, "Alessandro Grandi: A Case Study in the Choice of Texts for Motets," *Journal of the Royal Musical Association*, vol. 113, no.2 (1988): p. 282.

[26] Ibid., 278.

[27] According to Dietrich Bartel seventeenth-century theorists agree that "the dissonance of the semitone is considered useful for portraying the sadder affection, not only on account of its 'imperfect' and 'dissonant' proportion but also because of its small scope or span," in Dietrich Bartel. *Musica Poetica. Musical-Rhetorical Figures in German Baroque Music* (Lincoln and London: University of Nebraska Press, 1997), p. 49. French early modern

chromaticism – as opposed to functional harmony – will also be responsible for the "degradation" of tonal system. As in late sixteenth- and early seventeenth-century madrigals, twentieth-century chromaticism is of melodic origin, and it has little to do with nineteenth-century chromatic relationships between chords in functional harmony. If we follow the developmental thread of this phenomenon in Western tradition, its emotional range always incorporates expressions of strained innerness that could be described, in very general terms, as sorrowful, somber, or anxious.[28]

The rhetoric that Grandi gives to Jeremiah has something deeply human, and if ones wishes, something profoundly existential about it: its emotional and affective potential. The sonically and visually represented "lost self" seems very modern in its individualism and its detachment from its surroundings. It is the feeling that in *Erwartung* becomes nearly unbearable and that could be summed up in one word – alienation. Alienation (a recurrent theme throughout modernity),[29] defined by Hauser as *the loss of the wholeness*, seems as unsurpassed for the description of Michelangelo's and Grandi's characters. Hauser finds it in Don Juan, Faust, Don Quixote, and other fictional heroes of the period, as well as in the real-life neurosis of Tasso and Lasso, the depressions of Pontormo and Rossi, and the melancholy of numerous others.[30] *O Vos Omnes* shows that the agony of emotionally tortured individuality, as yet another modern trope, is equally present in the Christian ideology.

---

theorist Marin Mersenne (1558–1648), for example, claimed that: "Semitones or sharps represent tears, moans, because of their small intervals which express weakness, since small intervals as they ascend and descend are like children, old people, and those recovered from the long illness." See in Emilia Fadini, "The Rhetorical Aspect of Frescobaldi's Musical Language," in Alexander Silbiger (ed.), *Frescobaldi Studies: Sources of Music and Their Interpretation*, (Durham: Duke University Press, 1987), p. 292.

[28]   The chromatic descending melody becomes one of the main rhetorical figures in expressing lamentation throughout the Baroque: Carissimi uses this trope throughout his oratorio *Jepthe*; descending semitone opens Monteverdi's *Lamento d'Ariana* and builds the entire vocal phrase of Hecuba's lament in Cavalli's *Didone*; in Stradella's oratorio *San Giovanni Battista*, when Salome wants to seduce Herod she simulates lament, and opens her aria *Queste lagrime* with a descending semitone; furthermore, the chromatic descending tetrachord (*passus durisculus* according to Christoph Berhnard's terminology or *chromatic catabasis* in Athanasius Kircher's) becomes a manner of signifying lamentation in Venetian opera; we find it in the previously mentioned aria of Hecuba of Cavalli's *Didone*; even Purcell, in his *Dido and Aeneas*, "borrows" this rhetorical device in order to depict Dido's sorrow. Chromaticism depicts sorrow or other more somber moods and emotions in many works of modern Western art music, including those of Bach.

[29]   While Hegel understands alienation as a positive trans-historical category necessary for the development of the mind, Marx connects it to a historically defined period of Western history in which capital and reification dominate human relationships.

[30]   Hauser, p. 121.

Divine Encounters: Beyond Otherness

The state of "being only with oneself" was represented in art and music long before Schoenberg's nihilistic description. The early modern sense of "undivided" existence to which I now turn, though, is quite different, for it describes the possibility of oneness as experienced through a unity with God. In both cases, however, the subject is isolated from its surroundings. The absence of otherness in representations of divine love speaks about the isolation that, although tormenting, leads toward inner bliss. By contrast, expressionistic isolation is irreparable, characterizing a subject who cannot find the way toward either self or other.

In my discussion so far, noticeable is a certain paradox between the thesis that expressive art was welcomed and endorsed by the Church, while it simultaneously testified to deeply disturbed subjectivities. Our contemporary notion of art used as a political tool claims that it supports power structures by projecting some kind of social utopia and by evoking the pleasurable feelings of a contented subjectivity. However, early modern art tells quite a different story.[31]

But this is yet another paradox (as we would at least have it today) of confluence between the sacred and secular in early modern Europe. Another one is the notion that divine love (supposed unity with God) becomes metaphorically represented in a very "earthly" manner that does not deny the physical body. On the contrary, physical experience becomes used as the main metaphor that "translates" the state of divine union to quite effable terms. De Certeau explains this equation between erotic love and spiritual devotion in the sixteenth and seventeenth centuries as a "nostalgia" that originated from the progressive decline of God as the only object of love. The secularization of post thirteenth-century society, in his opinion, resulted in a change in the focus of love from the religious to the erotic (woman).[32] Mystics who searched for the new paths of religious devotion positioned the body at the center of their religious experiences as the only medium that could reach divine truth. Contemplation and prayer became issues of bodily pleasure and pain, much as in erotic love.

---

[31]   Maybe not so different, after all: the most successful and persistent political regimes have allowed freedom of artistic expression in order to prove their tolerance. The wrong assumption would be that they somehow did not recognize the political relevance of art; they only wanted to use it as a vehicle for positive propaganda. However, this is always a slippery terrain because art "behaves" unexpectedly, sometimes causing unintended reactions. As Foucault concludes: power never resides only at the top of the hierarchical structure as some kind of Leviathan (in his lectures at the College de France, Foucault refers to Thomas Hobbes's seminal work), but it always circulates in various ways through social and political structures. Thus, there's always a factor of surprise in how music is understood and appreciated.

[32]   Michel de Certeau, *The Mystic Fable: The Sixteenth and Seventeenth Centuries*, vol. 1, trans. Michael B. Smith (Chicago: University of Chicago Press, 1992), p. 4.

Even though based in part on the Song of Songs, this kind of religiosity did not always fit very well in Christian doctrines of spiritual devotion. With the rise of the Counter-Reformation, however, mystics, often regarded as renegades of official Christian dogmas, became the central proponents of Catholicism. This phenomenon raises several cultural issues. For example, the rethinking of peripheral influences on European Christianity, most notably those from the Iberian Peninsula and the Arab world. In Catholicism, the term "mystic" was not used as a noun until the sixteenth century when theologians began to propagate the privileged notion of union attained by few.[33]

Besides customary references to the influences of Platonic and Neoplatonic traditions on later mystic traditions, the paths of sixteenth-century divine love in the experiences of visionaries such as John of the Cross and Teresa of Avila can be traced in non-Christian contexts, especially to Islam. Mystical union described in Sufi poetry as the loss of reason, identity, and sense of self in the service of devotion closely resembles the experiences of Spanish visionaries. As Certeau explains, Spanish mystical writings are more than likely, directly or indirectly, influenced by Sufi's poetic equations between erotic and spiritual love.

The influence of mystical teachings manifests itself in musical representations of humans reaching toward the divine. In Benedetto Ferrari's *Cantata Spirituale* (1637), for example, the joyous musical affect metaphorically represents a state of religious devotion. The cantata has four parts, each of them comprising a strophe and refrain. The text of the first and the last part illustrates vivid imagery used by the poet, Ottavio Orsucci:

Those sharp thorns
Which you foster and nurture
In the forests of the abyss,
Afflict and wound,
Oh cruelty!
My Lord, my God.
They, the divine arrows,
Are beaten down and tempered
With the Heaven-borne fire,
They charm and sooth,
Oh, great mercy!
The devout and faithful heart.
And you, my soul,
Do you not recognize suffering,
Do you not yet feel love?

---

[33] On the history of mysticism, see Louis Dupré, "Unio Mystica: The State and the Experience," in Moshe Idel and Bernard McGinn (eds), *Mystical Union in Judaism, Christianity and Islam, (An Ecumenical Dialogue)* (New York: Continuum, 1999), pp. 3–23.

So, will that be your way
To live without love, without pain?
No, no, turn your heart,
Pleasing and meek,
O blessed fervour!
Towards such grievous agonies.
And with due reverence,
Repentant and in tears,
Exhale from our breast
The most fervent, the sweetest
Sentiments and sighs of love.
Thus, my soul,
You will recognize suffering,
And you will understand love.[34]

The strophes are set in a very common manner: the continuo only repeats a descending major tetrachord while the voice constantly improvises a melody. Unlike laments set similarly but over the minor tetrachord, the movement of a descent in major produces a pleasurable affect, and its repetition creates an open-ended loop that could last indefinitely and prolong the pleasure. It has been widely speculated that Benedetto Ferrari actually wrote the famous love duet "Pur ti miro, pur ti godo" that concludes Monteverdi's *L'incoronazione di Poppea*. That seems even more likely when taking into account the harmony and structure of *Cantata Spirituale and* comparing it to *Pur ti miro*. The descending ground-bass is identical, and although the duet has a significantly different texture from that of the solo cantata, the melodic principle is the same: improvisation over the ground bass. The duet is emotionally certainly more tense because of all the interval overlaps and suspensions between the voices; the lack of the voice of the other in the cantata, however, does not entirely lessen the expressiveness; it actually allows more freedom for simulating improvisatory style.

The refrain of the *Spiritual cantata*, on the other hand, is musically contrasting, written in a free, recitative style. It is more disturbing, as suggested by the narrative content and the rhetoric of the question asked (*Do you not yet feel love?*) And although the fourth part of the cantata brings about a promise (*And you will understand love*), the music stays the same: the dark-colored descending melody concludes the refrain and the entire piece.

---

[34]   *Queste pungenti spine/ che nei boschi d'abisso/ nudrite ed'allevate/ affliggono trafiggono/ o crudelate/ il mio Signor e dio// Son saette divine/ che col foco del cielo/ addolcite e temprate/allettano dilettano/ o gran pietate/ il cor divino e pio// E tu anima mia/ non sai che sia dolore/ ancor non senti amore?// Cosi dunque vivrai/ senz'amor senza duolo/ nò nò rivolgi il core/ pieghevole piacevole/ o buon fervore/ a si gravi martiri// E riverente homai/ pentita e lagrimosa/ manda dal petto fuore/caldissimi dolcissimi/ d'amor sensi e sospiri// Cosi anima mia/ saprai che sia dolore/ intenderai amore.*

Ferarri's cantata is internally conflicted, rhetorically speaking: it contains an expression of pleasure in the strophes against the musical and lyrical representation of pain in the refrain, and this juxtaposition of radically different emotions becomes reiterated throughout the text (*Do you recognize not suffering, Do you not yet feel love ... To live without love, without pain?*). Although the expressive refrain repeats several times, its final repetition does not resolve the tension already familiar from the refrain's first exposition. Like Grandi's *O Vos Omnes*, it leaves only the feeling of emotional exhaustion behind.

The feeling of pleasure and joy prevails in simulations of divine encounters, but as shown above, it is not necessarily represented by goal-oriented musical dramaturgy. On the contrary, as we have seen in the *Spiritual cantata*, the pleasurable conclusion is denied. As explained in the writings of St. Teresa of Avila, we do not learn to love God in a short time: prayer needs to become more dedicated if we want to reach mystical unity. Composers musically depict a state similar to ascending through the stages of spiritual enhancement of St. Teresa's "interior castle" or Muhammad's cosmos of the concentric spheres as described in Sufi writings.

This moment of denial is never more emphasized than in the devotional works of Heinrich Schütz. He spent most of his career as the Kapellmeister at the Dresden court, but he visited Italy on two occasions. In the previous chapter I already demonstrated how well he adopted the Italian style that was so appreciated at the Saxon court.[35]

In the concerto *O Süsser, o freundlicher, o gütiger Herr Jesu Christ* (*O sweet, o kindly, o good Lord Jesus Christ*), Schütz depicts the mystic encounter of the subject with God.[36] The introductory contemplation, invoking the Christ through words *O sweet, o kindly*, presents a slippery chromatic soundscape. After only two chords of presumably B♭ major, the voice starts to ascend chromatically, and continues a chromatic rise by the end of the phrase. Already in the fourth measure (*O good Lord Jesus Christ*) we are back in the "regular" tone of B♭ major as if nothing had happened at the very beginning. The introduction represents the flaw – the discursive disorientation of the subject, whether in despair or in the ecstasy of hope. It also represents the discursive space that needs to be somehow "corrected." In any case, it announces the main structural principle of the piece: the musical

---

[35] The years between 1609 and 1612 Schütz spent in Venice studying composition with Giovanni Gabrieli, and in 1628–29 he visited Claudio Monteverdi. In 1633, he wrote: "During my recent journey to Italy I engaged myself in a singular manner of composition, namely how a comedy of diverse voices can be translated into declamatory style and be brought to the stage and enacted in song – things that to the best of my knowledge are still completely unknown in Germany." Joshua Rifkin and Eva Linfield. "Schütz, Heinrich," *Grove Music Online*, L. Macy (ed.), http://www.grovemusic.com (accessed May, 13 2007).
[36] The concerto was published in the *Small Sacred Concertos* (*Kleine geistliche Concerte*) for voices and continuo (1636/1639).

development through ascending, which symbolizes the moment of contemplation and achievement of unity with Christ.

In the continuation, the subject, after addressing the Jesus, begins with his praise. Every sentence "opens" a new circle of sequences: *How greatly have you loved us wretched men* (F–C), *How dearly have you redeemed us* (G–D), *How lovingly have you comforted us* (*... wie hoch hast du uns elende Menschen geliebet, wie teur hast du uns erlöstet, wie lieblich hast du uns getröstet ... wie gewaltig hast du uns erhoben*) (A–E). The next phrase *How mightily have you exalted us* (*... wie gewaltig hast du uns erhoben ...*) musically leads towards the climax: a strange digression into the sphere of D that opens a new and unrecognized tonal sphere. In the first phrase of the sequence, though, Schütz reveals the reason for the necessity of contemplation and prayer: on the words *us wretched men*, the voice unexpectedly slides into the minor third.

But then when the direction of melody changes (*When I think of you, the kindlier you are, the greater is my love for you ... / wenn ich daran gedenke ... je freundlicher du bist, je lieber ich dich habe.*), the subject declares love, but not in ecstasy. Ascending into the realm of G hypodorian – the final tonal destination in the piece, as we will see later on – the subject achieves the unity in peace rather then in rapture.

The second verse starts with the subject's static praise of Lord: the harmonic rhythm is very slow and the voice is articulated in a quasi recitative style. *How wondrous is your charity which you have wrought for us/How great is the splendor which you have prepared for us* (*Mein Erlöser, wie herrlich sind deine Wohltaten, die du uns erzeiget hast*). On each of these laudations the harmonic rhythm gets faster, with the series of suspensions in voice and accompaniment that depict the excitement of the expectation of the mystic encounter. What follows is the first truly ecstatic moment, on the words *O how my soul longs for you* (*O wie verlanget meiner Seelen nach dir ...*). Long melisma (*O*) is not merely a melodic ornament: it ranges more then one ascending octave with a significant pause or a sigh in the very middle. The rhetoric move of ascending sequence is repeated again, confirming the main constructive principle of the entire piece. But the verse ends in G (with the Picardy third) connecting again rather different types of religious dedication: rapture and humility.

Finally, in the last verse (*My helper, you have ensnared my heart with your love/ Mein Helfer, du hast mir mein Herz genommen mit deiner Liebe ...*), the voice persistently repeats C♯ (that signifies the ascension throughout the piece) while the static accompaniment emphasizes the affect. Here, the effect of destabilization can be compared with the introductory chromaticism: it simultaneously signifies the emotions of grief and striving. The very last words are a strange kind of rejoicing. The verse *Ah, that I may soon come unto you and gaze upon your glory* (*... dass ich bald zu dir kommen und deine Herrlichkeit schauen sollte*) musically bears an equal amount of joy and urgency. It is a rejoicing hymn, but at the same time it preserves the affect of yearning. The emphasis on the sigh – the half note on "Ah" followed by a short pause and another "ah" – musically evokes the body that sighs.

The final repetition of the phrase begins with a vocal élan (the leap of fifth), but finishes modestly in G with a Picardy third. And indeed, the semantics of these final words carry a double meaning in the emotions of hope (*I may soon come unto you*) and admiration (*to gaze upon your glory*). Schütz unites the flourishing melody of the Italian Baroque with Lutheran piety, and even more strongly demonstrates the antithetical affects manifested in Ferrari's *Spiritual Cantata*.

The notion that precisely music, because of its non-discursive character, can somehow reach otherwise unreachable spheres of being became dominant only in the nineteenth century. The reversal from "religious music" to "music as religion," from its functional to aesthetic purpose, meant that music not only could but ought to mediate what other arts are incapable of. All (post)nineteenth-century spiritual music ended up in the realm where the art was not the means but the goal, the new religion itself. So when Messiaen and Scriabin try to reestablish a musical sensibility that would include a sense of spirituality, it is very much so with the reinvention and originality that belongs to the post-romantic notion of the artist who is actually a priest, a holy figure who offers redemption through music.[37] In Adorno's words: "Every music that aims at totality as a simile of the absolute has its theological dimension, even if it is unaware of it and even if it becomes anti-theological by virtue of presenting itself as a creation."[38] This creative model is something that Schoenberg inherited but also struggled with when composing "purely" religious works. Although he takes stories from the Bible, his dilemmas are contemporary: how to preserve (or discover) spirituality in times of the crisis of individuality. How to reconcile creation with Creation?

The Unutterable Silence: Representing the Ineffable

Early modern subjectivity was not liberated from ideas about the religious, nor from the mystical and metaphysical for that matter, for such matters continue to inform our contemporary subjectivity. The "discovery of man" did not bring about the secularization of all the worldviews; the process took place gradually, and even today it is felt differently in the various parts of the Western world. Twentieth-century revivals of "alternative" religions ("alternative" in relation to contemporaneous dominant Christianity), and twenty-first century religious radicalisms have stirred a new wave of discussion about religion: is religion unavoidable in discussions of contemporary society? Was it ever actually rooted out from modern Western culture? How do we understand new forms of religiosity?

---

[37] Scriabin in his *Poem of Ecstasy*, for example, concludes with a *tutti Maestoso* orchestra that represents spiritual ascension. It is Scriabin who enables transcendence through music. The fear of representing disappears once the artist retakes the role of the prophet.

[38] Adorno, p. 234.

If we take into consideration music, the representation of transcendental states – either related to official religious dogmas or understood as aesthetic experiences – was always an issue with which composers grappled. Even in the case of Schoenberg, whose systematic and rationalistic methods – revolutionary contributions to twentieth-century music – are focal points of musicological interest, matters of spirituality and religion never lost their primacy. Very much outside the frame of any religious tradition, he was, like the main character in *Erwartung*, always looking for something beyond the mere nihilism that he sensed as a predominant feeling of his time.

Although he returned repeatedly to such themes over the course of his life, however, Schoenberg never managed to solve the problem of representing religious devotion in music. Although not unsuccessful, his works concerned with the possible recovery of faith – the oratorio *Die Jakobsleiter* (1917) and the opera *Moses und Aron* (1930–32) – were never brought to an end, despite his perpetual attempts at finishing them.

The choice to discuss Schoenberg's religious compositions may seem unrelated to my introductory discussion on *Erwartung*. All of these works, however, despite their generic differences, are deeply related by the sense that they continue, negotiate, and significantly negate canonical modes of musical representation. This point of view enables us to understand why Schoenberg decided to perform one of his religious meditations in the operatic genre. Slavoj Žižek explains:

> [W]hile *Parsifal* retains a full naive trust in the (redemptive) power of music and finds no problems in rendering the noumenal divine dimension in the aesthetic spectacle of the ritual, *Moses und Aaron* attempts the impossible: to be an opera directed against the very principle of opera, that of the stage-musical spectacle – it is an operatic representation of the Jewish prohibition of aesthetic representation.[39]

While I agree that opera in Wagner's hands, as in the works of Messiaen and Scriabin, becomes the vehicle of a religious restoration though aesthetic transcendence, I don't think that Schoenberg's inability to finish his religious meditations has to do exclusively with the prohibition of representation in the faith he embraced rather late in his life. Schoenberg's problems in musical representation speak more to the general sense of nihilism I tried to demonstrate in relation to *Erwartung*.

But let us proceed chronologically. It took Schoenberg years to finish first the text and then only partially music to his oratorio *Die Jakobsleiter*. The problems, related to everyday political conditions, as well as to his creative uncertainties as to how to approach to this kind of work, interfered with the final execution.

---

[39]   Slavoj Žižek, "The Politics of Redemption: Why is Wagner Worth Saving?" *Journal of Philosophy and Scripture* (Fall 2004), http://www.lacan.com/zizred.htm (accessed May 13, 2007).

But besides the disruptive events that prevented the finishing of *Die Jakobsleiter* (the First World War and the military draft), it was Schoenberg himself who kept changing his ideas about the oratorio's ideal sound. Yet he kept coming back to this work, in the hope that he would find the best solution for its final version.[40]

The roots of this indecisiveness originate from the general cultural climate, but also from very specific conditions of Schoenberg's personal background. He was born and raised in a secular family, and when he felt a need to tackle the questions of spirituality, he was not strongly attached to any particular dogma.[41] Consequently, he created an amalgam of various beliefs and religious views influenced by mysticism, literature, and theosophy.[42]

Die Jakobsleiter is, like *Erwartung*, a process of soul-searching. In *Erwartung*, the main character is just called "the woman," and the oratorio's main characters are also impersonal: *Gabriel, one who is called, one who is rebellious, one who is struggling, he who is chosen, The Monk, He who is dying, Soul*. In contrast to *Erwartung*, however, Schoenberg wants in *Die Jakobsleiter* to find some sort of redemption, something outside the self in order to repair the obviously damaged state of the soul and the world altogether. At a time of prevalent nihilism, he wanted to go beyond its reiteration – which is what *Erwartung* is all about. The introductory uncertainty of the woman's questioning in *Erwartung* (*Go in there?. I can't see the path* ...), becomes not less uncertain but more comforting at the beginning of *Die Jakobsleiter*. The archangel Gabriel opens the oratorio with: *Whether to right or left, forward or back, uphill or down, one must go on, without asking what lies ahead or behind* (*Ob rechts, ob links, vorwärts oder rückwärts, bergrauf oder begrab – man hat weiter-zugeben, ohne fragen, was vor oder hinter einem liegt*). The reconciling rhetoric of *Die Jakobsleiter* already reveals the intention, if not to conclude, then at least to proceed.

But precisely this poses his biggest challenge: to find the musical equivalent of the metaphorical connection – the ladder that connect heaven and earth in Jacob's dream (The Book of Genesis, 28:10). How to represent musically the prayer that could offer redemption? And Schoenberg does not offer an easy solution. If the

---

[40]   Which is actually the right version of *Die Jakobsleiter*? On Zillig's intervention and the power of Boulez's performance in the perception history of this oratorio, see Jennifer Shaw, "New Performance Sources and Old Modernist Productions, 'Die Jakobsleiter' in the Age of Mechanical Reproduction," *The Journal of Musicology*, vol. 19, no.3 (Summer, 2002): pp. 434–460.

[41]   He set poetry saturated in conventional Catholic imagery, for example, to signify an entirely non-devotional sense of decadence in *Pierrot Lunaire* (songs *Madonna, Red mass*, and the *Crosses*).

[42]   Schoenberg was strongly influenced by Balzac's philosophical tales. John Covach traces Balzac's spirituality to the work of Swedish scientist and theologian Emanuel Swedenborg, and he also discusses the influence of Goethe and Schopenhauer on Schoenberg's sacred works. John Covach, "The Sources of Schoenberg's 'Aesthetic Theology'," *19th-Century Music*, vol. 19, no. 3 (Spring, 1996): pp. 252–262.

archangel's words are full of promise, the choir expresses the same confusion as the only character in *Erwartung*: *Onward? Whither? How long?* (*Weiter? Wohin? Wie lange?*) *The malcontents* complain, *the doubters* question, *the rejoicers* celebrate, and *the indifferent* and *the quietly resigned* disinterestingly proceed. *The beauty seeker*, *the rebellious*, *the struggling*, *the chosen one* (presumably the artist himself), *the monk*, and *the dying* – they all, unable to find the path to inner peace, have words of complaint for Gabriel.

Gabriel's final response (to the dying) is actually a description of the moment of transcendence to the other side of the known. It's the moment of guidance in which Gabriel promises final enlightenment while the Soul, represented by the high female vocalization, accompanies him. The moment of transcendence is represented musically by the transition from verbalization to vocalization, from rhetorically guided expression to abstract utterance: the final sigh of the Dying is transformed into the high voice of his Soul. The very last number is an extended symphonic interlude with the high female voices and a soprano (*the Soul*). At this point, Schoenberg decides to experiment with the potentials of the performing space, and he assigns ensembles that would play from a "high" position and from afar.[43] His experimentation is inspired by a need to describe the non-describable, and at this point, he not only leaves the traditional means of representation, but he also makes the music "leave" the stage in order to depict the beyond-the-ordinary experience of spiritual transcendence.

No matter how much he tries to abandon traditional musical rhetoric, however, Schoenberg is still imprisoned by it, because he wants to present its negation (vocalization instead of wording), and by negating it, he actually reiterates its relevance: he moves in an already prescribed circle defined by the dialectics of (non)representation. Unlike the composers of electro-acoustic experiments that I discussed in the previous chapter, he cannot entirely break with the traditional language that is simultaneously the source of his creative frustration and his guiding force. And nowhere is that more obvious than at the very conclusion of *Die Jakobsleiter*: as the stage orchestra dies out in *piano*, and the orchestra and high female voices dominate from outside the stage, the soprano who is placed at the high position echoes the *Soul* (the soprano from afar). The two voices that reflect each other conclude the first part of the oratorio, offering the off-stage space (*high above – afar*) as the only possible way to represent transcendence. This is a reiteration of the concept of space that I discussed in the first chapter when describing Bernini's St. Teresa: the included surrounding spaces never actually manage to overpower the centralistic status of the stage. Where to move from here? The only way is to leave standard representational tools altogether and to create, as Schoenberg tried to do, a system that entirely defies them. This paradoxical state of the impossible conclusion seems to many almost a perfect solution, best

---

[43] He was very concerned as to how the off-stage groups (*Fernmusik*) would function in performing venues. Towards the end of his life, he even had the idea of using acoustically isolated rooms and microphone transmission for performing this part of the score.

described by Schoenberg's pupil Winfried Zillig (1905–1963) who prepared the oratorio's performance score:

> Strangely enough, the conclusion of the "Jacob's Ladder" fragment is one of the most impressive endings in the whole of Occidental music. Schönberg's invention of sounds floating in space does in fact lead to new regions. The enchantment is complete despite the fragmentary character. Indeed, one cannot help thinking that this strange and unique enchantment arises directly from the work's unfinished state; for such a work, given its intellectual premise, can provide only an incomplete answer in view of mankind's limitations when facing the eternal.[44]

Schoenberg's relationship with space is a mirror-image of his relationship with tonality. Although he struggled with the problem of *Fernmusik* in this piece, he did not actually continue his exploration in this direction. For, dealing with tonality offered much more room for the exercise of negative dialectics than did his spatial experiments with music. I will not get into a discussion of the 12-tone system and its potential for reviving Western musical creativity. The truth is, however, that, Schoenberg gradually changed his musical language, and that works like *Erwartung* and *Die Jakobsleiter* show the tendency towards 12-note organization that harmonically and melodically negates any kind of traditional musical development. If the exposition of all 12 tones was "hidden" in the introduction to the monodrama because of the accent on textural verticality and the exploitation of instrumental color, it is very open at the beginning of the oratorio: the six-tone ostinato in the violoncellos (C♯, D, F, E, G♯, G) is gradually complemented with the layering of the rest of the chromatic scale (C, E♭, B, B♭, F♯, A).

As we have seen, however, the problem of musical representation of a truth that lies beyond earthly cognition seems to be problematic from the very beginnings of "representational" music. Schoenberg only inherited one of the oldest problems in musical representation. I have already shown that the musical simulation of ecstatic states rarely follows goal-oriented dramaturgy. The same could be said of early modern pieces that deal with the descriptions of the divine.

In his Latin oratorio *Judicium extremum*, Giacomo Carissimi musically represents, as the title suggests, the Day of Judgment (Matthew: 24, 25). Like Michelangelo, he describes the promise of the end and the dread it causes among humans. Carissimi concludes the oratorio with ascending tonal regions: *The springs will dry up* (D), *the rivers will dry up* (E), *the seas will dry up* (F), *the palace of heaven will fall* (G), *the engine of the world will collapse* (A) – *Arescent fontes, arescent flumina, arescent aequora, caeli regia concidet, mundi machina corruet*. In setting the final words, however, Carissimi decides to conclude the piece (by repeating the verb *collapse*) in the home key of G. After the tension

---

[44] Rudolph Stephan, Preface to the score of *Jacob's Ladder* by Arnold Schoenberg (Universal Edition: 1980).

created by ascending movement, the "proper" conclusion on the final G sounds like a retreat. The very concept of an ascending conclusion seems impossible to perform satisfactorily because the every new key area becomes conquered with a leading tone. In this sense, there is no key to strive for, and the only possible solution is a never-ending sequence or a modulating loop that would continue as far as the register limits would allow. Another possibility for concluding might have involved some kind of musical and dramatic shift, with a different tonal strategy that would have broken out of this infinite regress. The end of the oratorio as it is – confirming G (V–I) after a gradual and tense ascension towards the A area – suggests that musical rhetoric cannot really satisfactorily represent "the collapse" as the final act of God. In this context, the ending of the world and the last moment of mankind are depicted in the only possible way: by denying representation.

I have already pointed out that early modern and late modern senses of the "musical religious" very much differ from romantic ones. In essence, early and late modern composers felt fear in front of the possibility of representation precisely because of the fact that they were aware that music "signifies." Many romantic composers believed that music does not represent but *is* a religious state. And Schoenberg's requestioning of musical conventions led him to doubt this romantic agenda, going back to very beginnings of modern musical representation, and posing similar questions to those of his early modern predecessors who established norms in the first place.

Let us turn once again to Schoenberg's experiments in this field. He "continues" the exploration he has begun in *Die Jakobsleiter* in his religious opera *Moses und Aron*, albeit now completely applying the 12-tone system. The opera begins with vocalization (six solo voices placed in the orchestra) like the one that concludes *Die Jakobsleiter*. It describes the sound "from behind" the knowledge.[45] But immediately after that, Schoenberg sets up another dialectical relationship: the *Voice from the Burning Bush* (*speaking* voices) echoes the *singing* of the soloists from the orchestra. Besides creating an eerie effect that is very similar to (but much more dissonant than) Schütz's representation of the persecution of Saul, Schoenberg immediately juxtaposes musical representation (singing) and its negation (speech) – a distinction repeated in the juxtaposition of the speaking role of Moses to the singing one of Aaron. Moses is the one who knows (like the

---

[45]   To go back to Žižek's previous remark about the opera: although *Moses und Aron* deals with the issues from the collective past of the Jewish people, I believe that Schoenberg wants to tackle a more universal set of issues in it. I agree with John Bokina that: "at a deeper level, *Moses* is not so much about the geographical transition of a people from one place to another as it is about a spiritual growth of a people from a lower stage of consciousness and civilization to a higher. At this level, *Moses* transcends the Jewish–Nazi nexus. It becomes an allegory about the emancipatory potential of enlightened human beings." John Bokina, "Resignation, Retreat, and Impotence: The Aesthetics and Politics of the Modern German Artist-Opera," *Cultural Critique*, no. 9 (Spring, 1988): p. 183.

artist) but is not capable of expressing himself in an understandable way. That is why he uses Aaron as a mediator who is, unlike Moses's with his speaking vocal part, capable of musical signification. This relationship between words and music may seem paradoxical: the divine is signified by ordinary speech while the earthly is signified by music, but in the context of Schoenberg's dilemma with musical representation, it is quite consistent. There is no music that can describe divinity, and speech takes the place of the mediator of the indescribable. Schoenberg replicates this very non-romantic turnaround in musical signification in the second scene in which Moses meets his brother in the Wasteland. Aaron's *grazioso*, heroic tenor part musically represents the opposition to Moses' speech, reflecting its rhetoric like a reverse image. They simultaneously sing and speak: *O vision of highest fantasy, how glad it is that you've enticed it to form you!* (Aaron) *How can fantasy thus picture the unimaginable?* (Moses) – *Gebilde der höchsten Phantasie, wie dankt sie dir's, dass du sie reizest zu bilden* (Aron). *Kein Bild kann dir ein Bild geben vom Unvorstellbaren* (Moses).

The entire opera revolves around the dilemma of whether prophets should try to prove the existence of the Almighty, or should employ some other means of persuasion that avoids idolatry. In the second act, Aaron fulfills people needs for a material proof of the divinity (the scene with the golden calf) while Moses despairs because of his brother's ways. At the very end of the second act, Moses exclaims: "O word, thou word, that I lack!" complaining about his inability to persuade his people about the God's existence. And this is the point at which the opera finishes. Just before his death, however, Schoenberg allowed the third act to be read. He obviously wanted to conclude differently by reaching the final words of the third act: "unity with God." The lack of words, the inability of music to represent that would describe divine unity here becomes literal. If in early modern pieces this was a rhetorical move, in Schoenberg's poetics, this inability translates into his working process.

By going back once again to early modern sources, I will once more explain what I exactly mean by rhetorically performed lack of expression. Alessandro Grandi's motet *Plorabo die ac nocte* (*Day and night I shall cry*, 1616), for instance, concludes with the only example of discursive break-down that I know in modern music. As in the previously discussed motet *O Vos Omnes*, Grandi combines the text from the most various sources: some verses are taken from the Old and New Testament, and some are completely unrecognizable; and all this with a particular goal in mind: to create a narrative that is powerful enough to depict the scene of a collective lament.

> Day and night I shall cry for the prince of my people who has been killed.
> For what is there for me in heaven, and what did I wish for thee on earth?
> See, all ye people, if there is any sorrow like my sorrow.
> My soul refuses to be comforted because they have taken away my Lord,
> And I know not where they have placed him.
> Night and day I shall cry for the prince of my people who has been killed.

How was it that Thou, strong in battle, were struck and killed?
I shall lament for Thee, my good Jesus, so becoming and so kind.
See, all ye people, if there is any sorrow like my sorrow.
O Jesus, my Son, who may grant that I may die for Thee?
And all people know it,
Because there is any sorrow like my sorrow.[46]

    I can only speculate about the identities of the members of this lamenting group: it probably involves Jesus's disciples and Mary Magdalene. The text in the canto, however, directly refers to Mary who sings "O Jesu, fili mi." At the very end, however, instead of "Jesu," she manages only to voice the first syllable "Je-." Her pain depicts almost physical suffering: she weeps until she loses herself. Grandi creates a very theatrical representation of the lamenting of Jesus by leaving the concluding word of the motet unfinished. His maneuver is even more emphasized because the other three voices properly conclude the motet.[47]

    But this rhetorical collapse at the very end of the motet has been prepared from its very beginning. The lamenting declamation in Aeolian begins in the bass and then moves to the alto and tenor, the first time solo and then as a part of the group. The sequentially repeated descending short motives simulate the intonation of mourning. Mary (that is, the canto) begins to sing very late into the piece, but then her part dramatically fuels the rest of it. The descending motive of lamentation frenetically repeats, and although the canto seemingly closes the piece, the weeping (lamentation intersected by breaks) continues. Finally, whereas the other voices perform the expected closure in A, the canto loses itself in an agony of repetition, and "forgets" to conclude: its weeping stops on D (a seventh over the fifth degree), leaving the name of Jesus half unspoken. This rhetorical decision reveals the composer's intention to amaze and surprise and – quite contrary to elitist mannerisms – to address the most elementary human emotions, which are (let us remind ourselves once again of Panofsky's excellent definition) "humanly simple" or "simply human."

    But, as I previously explained, one of the goals of the Counter-Reformation was to propagate this kind of connection between religious piety and emotional responsiveness in order to reach the worshippers. The art like Grandi's was

---

[46]   *Plorabo die ac nocte interfectum principem populi mei./Quid enim mihi est in caelo, et a te quid volui super terram?/Videte omnes populi, si est dolor similis sicut dolor meus./ Renuet consolari anima mea quia tulerunt Dominum meum, nescio ubi posuerunt eum./ Plorabo die ac nocte interfectum principem populi mei./ Quomodo cecidisti fortis in proelio et occisus es?/ Dolebo, super te, mi bone Jesu, decore nimis et amabilis./ Videte omnes populi, si est dolor similis sicut dolor meus./ O Jesu, fili mi, quis mihi det ut ego moriar pro te?/ Et sciant omnes populi quia non est dolor similis sicut dolor meus.*

[47]   Roche compares this maneuver of closing the motet in lower voices (*sicut dolor tuus*-like your grief) to onlookers in Greek chorus fashion who comment on the main character's (in this case Mary's) destiny. Roche, p. 282.

officially supported and welcomed. Nonetheless, the representation of the final stage in these compositions always seems problematic. In the context of Grandi's motet, there are no words or sounds imaginable to represent Mary's suffering.

In early and late modern musical pieces that deal with the religious experience, the conclusion poses a problem. It seems that an adequate treatment of divine encounters and related emotional states in *stile rappresentativo* requires the denial of the very premises of representation. This becomes the burning question at the very beginning of the development of musical representation (how to depict divinity?), but also at the end of musical modernity. In the early period, this question was closely related to the politics of the church: representing divinity fitted very well with the general tendency of reestablishing the Catholic authority. In the post Enlightenment period that "suffered" from the ideals of humanism as it questioned them, this problem gained an entirely different dimension, most clearly shown in Schoenberg's work. From this perspective, Schoenberg not only asked questions related to the religious ineffable, but also to the ineffable created by man (artist) as an agent of the divine. In this sense, he is "going back to the roots" of the modern question of how to negotiate individuality and divinity. What are the boundaries of human, and where they intersect with the divine? It may seem that Schoenberg did not succeed in his intentions. But speaking in the terms of negative dialectics, his respect for the totality of musical work is precisely contained in the refusal to reproduce it. To compose "unity with god," as Gesualdo sensed so early on, would be a lie: the God of Western society has been long forgotten, and a man (an artist) is not, after all, capable of calling him back.

Chapter 3

The Terror of Desire:
Arbitrary Outcomes or the *Dei ex Machinis*

Between Tragedy and Comedy

Despite dramatic inconsistencies and a problematic "double" ending, the longevity of W.A. Mozart's *Don Giovanni*, one of the most powerful and most popular works still performed on the operatic stage, resides in its conflicting logic: the audience gets thrilled, again and again, with the arrogance that Don Giovanni shows as he faces death, even as it often remains skeptical towards the moral of the final ensemble. The alleged problem of *Don Giovanni* arises from a sort of *mistake* in the dramatization: the punishment of the main character does not come as a logical consequence of his originally positive musical characterization. That Mozart's sympathies were on the "wrong" side is quite obvious from his depiction of Don Giovanni as a man of instincts, the follower of his own passions, the embodiment of *joie de vivre*, the romantic hero who stands for his own ideals, the chevalier who fights and defends his honor. In spite of his admirable musical qualities, however, Don Giovanni in the end gets punished as a dangerous seducer and a violator of social rituals. In other words, Mozart shows an immense amount of sympathy for the character who seriously endangers the social order. He empowers him with all possible rhetorical guises, challenging the audience with the premise that beautiful does not necessarily mean good.[1] When a transgressor violates social norms, this transgression registers not only in the realm of musical rhetoric but also translated into a violation of how the musical story should go; in the case of opera, it breaks the norms of musical drama. More precisely, conventional genre expectations become betrayed: tragedy fails to bring about cathartic experiences of fear and pity, while comedy lacks happy endings. The version of *Don Giovanni*

---

[1] Some interpreters of Don Giovanni claim that the character lacks musical consistency, perhaps because, as an anti-hero, Don Giovanni does not deserve proper musical presentation. Mozart, however, has two ways of characterizing Don Giovanni: the first is the impersonal characterization of the *bon vivant* (as displayed in the *Champagne aria*) who loves everything that has to do with earthly pleasures, and everyone who shares the same love will be captured by it. The second is that of the seducer: he speaks what those that surround him want to hear. His main strategy, I believe, is to speak the language of others in order to win them over: folk-like simplicity with Zerlina, lyrical warmth with Donna Elvira, buffoonery with Leporello; Don Giovanni assumes their musical identities and uses them as if they were his own.

that excludes the final ensemble betrays both: in the first place, there is no final moral that "warns" the audience, and, more important, although Don Giovanni dies, he never repents.

Numerous retellings of the story of Don Juan embody a conflict between spirituality and sensuality – one of the most important conflicts of Western culture.[2] More specifically, the dissonance of Mozart's opera has to be read in the context of a subversion of eighteenth-century ideals. According to John Bokina, Don Giovanni represents the values of a feudal, aristocratic "style of baroque living" as opposed to the communal values (reason, stability, industriousness) of Enlightenment society.[3] But this opposition is not entirely clear; as Mladen Dolar lucidly notes, Don Giovanni embodies both "the old order of absolute privilege against which the Enlightenment's crusade is directed, and the autonomous subject which is the cornerstone of the Enlightenment."[4] Don Giovanni is not merely a precursor of romantic subjectivity, as music writers often claim. Most of the time he does not seem a subject at all; deprived of self-reflection, his characterization is caught up somewhere between premodern moral pragmaticism and liberal individualism. As a result, he does not fit into either of the two worldviews. It is as if a premodern hero enters the world of the Enlightened: the two worlds collide, and the catastrophe becomes unavoidable.[5]

---

[2]   The myth of a seducer who is punished for his sins permeates more than three centuries of our cultural history, resonating with very universal human qualities – desire, sensuality, eroticism. And the constant retelling of this story by many artists – Molière, Byron, Shaw, to name just a few – precisely shows how much the Christian world was (or is) confused with its own sensuality; how eroticism has imposed contradictory feelings on European subjectivity throughout the ages. Yet the attitude towards sensuality has changed over time: for pre-romantic audiences, the story of Don Juan or Don Giovanni is a moral story, a warning for tempted individuals. In romanticism, Don Giovanni is a favorite hero because he stands for the celebration of instincts and unbounded freedom, regardless of the consequences.

[3]   See John Bokina, "The Dialectic of Operatic Civilization: Mozart's Don Giovanni," in *Opera and Politics, from Monteverdi to Henze* (New Haven: Yale University Press, 1997), p. 43.

[4]   Mladen Dolar, "Don Giovanni," in Slavoj Žižek and Mladen Dolar, *Opera's Second Death* (New York and London: Routledge, 2002), p. 47.

[5]   Early reviews make it quite clear that Don Giovanni did not have an easy reception. After the Berlin premiere, the *Chronik von Berlin* reported: "If ever an opera has been awaited with eagerness, if ever a work of Mozart's has been exalted to the skies before it was heard, it was *Don Giovanni*! That Mozart is an outstanding, even a great composer, the whole world will admit; but that nothing greater than this opera has ever been written or ever will be – that we beg leave to doubt. Theatrical music knows no other rule, no other judge than the heart; that is the only criterion of its value. It is not excessive instrumentation that counts. The heart, feelings and passions are what the composer must articulate; then he will write something great, then his name will go down to posterity. Grétry, Monsigny and Philidor will prove this. In *Don Giovanni* Mozart wanted to write something extraordinary,

Whatever the case, Mozart's version of the myth, born of the ideas of the Enlightenment, is historically defined: once European culture recognized reason as the ruler of human behavior, every social endeavor had to be measured by it. But this is a dialectical relationship: the dominance of the reason always produces a sense of nostalgia for what has been lost in the process of realizing the self as primarily a rational being. And *Don Giovanni* plays the card of this nostalgia: what if? What if one forgets about social standing, civic duties, or Christian morals? It is a fantasy of a reason-constrained society that does not promise to fade away in the immediate future. What never stops to enthrall audiences is precisely its moral conflict: should we follow our desires, or should we fulfill communal duties in our pursuit of happiness? If we proceed instinctively, what if we hurt someone in the process? If we listen to our consciences and follow the rules of social conduct, will we ever feel free, unconstrained, and happy?

In Mozart's opera, however, the main character – almost a metaphor of the pleasure-principle, a non-person who projects a desire for individual transgression – is the only one who oversteps the bounds of moral norms. The world that surrounds him stays in the end unshattered by his moral violations.

In the context of my study, however, I am more interested in works that display a dilemma less often taken into account: what if the entire society comes to be governed only by human desire and the pleasure principle? What if desire corrupts everyone, leading the entire society to the brink of collapse? In this case, the entire community – not only one aberrant individual – is the transgressor. If in previous chapters I wanted to explain how newly-formed selfhood becomes reflective, how it explores its existential limits (literally, in physical space, and metaphorically – in the inner space of selfhood), now I want to see what kind of changes such self-empowerment brings in the outer space of social interaction, not from the individualistic perspective, but from the perspective of the entire community.

And yet again, my interest in this phenomenon springs from the discovery of fascinating similarities between early and late modern periods. In seventeenth-century works, the sense of social righteousness characteristic of Mozart's time had not yet been entirely formed. But that does not mean it was not counted as one of the most important questions of emerging modern identity. The awareness yielded by this politically and socially turbulent century started to work against the worldviews of harmonious existence as imagined by renaissance humanists.[6]

---

something inimitably great; certainly there is something extraordinary there, but nothing inimitably great! Whim, mood, pride, not the heart, created *Don Giovanni*, and we would rather be asked to admire the sublime possibilities in an oratorio or some other solemn church music of his than in this work." In Hermann Abert, *Mozart's Don Giovanni*, trans. Peter Gellhorn (London: Eulenburg Books, 1976), p. 20.

[6] Arnold Hauser seems right to conclude concerning modern fantasies of social utopia: "Apart from brief episodes, the complete harmony between subject and object, form and content, characteristic of antiquity and the Middle Ages, was never reached again."

The musical score that most profoundly displays this kind of awareness is Claudio Monteverdi's *L'incoronazione di Poppea* (1642). Its librettist, Giovanni Francesco Busenello (1598–1659), was a member of the group of Venetian patricians and intellectuals, the *Accademia degli Incogniti* (1630–1661), responsible for *Poppea* as well as for the creation of many other dramatic and operatic works. *Poppea* reveals the problems of a contemporary Venetian society: the old glory of Venice was slowly fading away, and the *Incogniti* were exploring the reasons for the decline of their proud Republic. They closely examined their own social and political dilemmas: the advantages of republic to monarchy (if any), the place and influence of women in society, the role of bodily pleasures in life.

Moreover, music created in the religious context of Rome reveals cultural perplexities very similar to the ones created by liberally minded Venetians. As I explained in the previous chapter, modernity was dealt with in both secular and sacred contexts; both theater and the church stage, in their own terms, displayed this significant change in mentality. And nothing proves that better than another seventeenth-century work I will discuss in this chapter, the oratorio *Saint John, the Baptist* (*San Giovanni Battista*, 1675) by Alessandro Stradella (1632–1682).

In general terms, these two seventeenth-century works examine human desire as a collective phenomenon that circulates through and shapes all of society. This non-individualistic perspective is fairly rare in modern drama, but it will resurface again as a major question in a historically crucial moment for twentieth-century Europe: in the between-the-wars phase of the German state, the Weimar Republic. The works by Kurt Weill and Bertolt Brecht – *The Threepenny Opera* (*Die Dreigroschenoper*, 1928) and *Rise and Fall of the City of Mahagonny* (*Aufstieg und Fall der Stadt Mahagonny*, 1930) – reiterate the early-modern dilemma about the repercussions of unconstrained human desire. Again, this desire relates to the whole of society; there are no privileged or spared ones who are somehow resistant to it. More important, their conclusions, like those of seventeenth-century works I examine, do not bring about catharsis.

In the avant-garde culture and artistic production of the Weimar Republic, the display of moral crises reaches its peak. There is anger at failures of the Enlightenment project and – as in Schoenberg's oeuvre – a proclamation: we failed as a civilization, and now we can only sing about this failure and reveal it in all its monstrosity. By doing so, artists are caught up in a loop of constant reiteration that European culture has reached a dead end. The pessimistic status quo and the critique of the Enlightenment that they cannot get away from, however, originate precisely from the heart of "Enlightened" thought: the fantasy of a possible humane utopia. As Schoenberg implies in his poetics, which I discussed in the previous chapter, there is no escape from this closed circle: to break it means to break with the ideals that formed it in the first place. But if Schoenberg's work operates within the closed circle of negative dialectics, the simultaneous continuation and critique

Arnold Hauser, *Mannerism: The Crisis of the Renaissance and the Origin of Modern Art*, translated by Eric Mosbacher (Cambridge: Harvard University Press, 1986), p. 6.

of expressionism in Weimar music-theater provoke heated controversy. When Weill and Brecht imagine an entire city grounded in social utopianism (curiously called Mahagonny), they go back to the early-modern concern with pleasure as a guiding force for the whole of the society. The controversial elements reside on several levels, but they stem in part from the disparity between the intentions of the librettist and those of the composer. Speaking in dramaturgical terms, Brecht and Weill divorce musical characterization from ethics: like their early-modern counterparts Monteverdi and Stradella, or like Mozart in *Don Giovanni*, they give beautiful music to ethically challenged characters.

No Hope, No Fear: Externalizing Desire

Opera, in both its early-modern beginnings and its numerous twentieth-century "deaths," is the genre that most transparently questions the status of musical drama, its purpose, and the ways music should "follow" the dramatic thread and participate in the complex net of expressive elements. How should stories end? Are there other ways to develop drama besides comedy and tragedy? What do these stories tell about the cultures from which they originate? Operatic scores are probably the most illuminating sources for the exploration of these phenomena. They are the richest archives of modernity – the multimedia traces of modern dilemmas.[7]

L'incoronazione di Poppea is the first opera that takes into account real historical events.[8] Busenello's main goal in retelling the historical events described in the *Annals* by the first-century Roman historian Cornelius Tacitus is to engage critically with contemporary reality.[9] In other words, although the

---

[7]   As I pointed out in the first chapter, opera is a true modern genre. Its beginnings around 1600 and the numerous proclamations of its symbolical death in the twentieth century conveniently coincide chronologically with the limits of the historical phenomenon I am interested in. The fact that opera represents the genre that composers just can't let go even today speaks a great deal about our contemporary relationship to the legacies of modernity: the obsession with fantasized representations and explorations of selfhood on a theater stage. In 1922, just two years before the creation of Puccini's *Turandot* and Berg's *Wozzeck*, a reference point that some music historians cite as a possible moment of opera's death, Busoni writes in opera's defense: "I expect that in the future the opera will be the chief, that is to say the universal and one form of musical expression and content." Ferruccio Busoni, "The Essence and Oneness of Music," *The Essence of Music and Other Papers*, trans. Rosamond Lay (London: Rockliff, 1957), p. 5. Busoni died in 1924, leaving his last opera, *Doktor Faustus*, unfinished.

[8]   See Peter N. Miller, "The Literary Sources," in Ian Fenlon and Peter N. Miller, *The Song of the Soul: Understanding 'Poppea'* (London: Royal Musical Association, 1992), p. 6.

[9]   Miller names several possible sources for Busenello's libretto: *Lives of the Caesars* by Suetonius (*c*.77–125), *Roman History* by Dio Cassius (*c*.170–230), *Annals* by

action of *Poppea* takes place in ancient Rome at the time of the emperor Nero, the opera's conflicts examine the Venetian state of affairs. The fact that Busenello freely (and oftentimes chronologically inaccurately) uses the Roman past reflects precisely this intention to use the mask of history in order to speak about the present.[10] From this point of view, it is not important to get the sequence of events right; it is more relevant to have all the necessary ingredients to tell the story of the (re)distribution of social and political power: the seductive and unscrupulous contenders to the throne (Poppea, Ottavia), the cruel, weak, and decadent ruler (Nero), the intellectual, contemplative force (philosopher Seneca), and the rest of the suite that is manipulated likewise by ambitions and desires (Poppea's lover Otho, her court maid Drusilla, servant Arnalta, and many other nameless courtiers and Romans). One thing is obvious: all the characters are "infected" by moral corruption. No one is innocent. While Poppea and Nero want to get rid of Ottavia in order to be together, Otho, Ottavia, and Drusilla want to kill Poppea and get their revenge. The most problematic status, however, is given to Seneca. He dies in the middle of the opera and the treatment of his character is, as we shall see, crucial for the understanding of *Poppea*.

The difficulty with the opera's often problematic reception arises from the fact that its characters are not portrayed either as right or wrong. They are not rewarded for their good deeds, nor are they punished for their crimes. Otho's sorrow does not become less sincere after his desperate attempt to kill Poppea, nor is Ottavia's strength somehow forgotten once she ends up banished from Rome. What kind of ruler is Nero? The subjected (the soldiers and a valet in Act One) say he is weak; his music says he is in love (in his duets with Poppea), and his deeds say he is cruel (he banishes his wife from Rome and orders Seneca's suicide). What about Seneca? Even if his words and music might be construed as those of a virtuous hero, the characters who surround him think and speak quite the opposite. Seneca is not a hero not only because his narration and music oftentimes demean him,

---

Tacitus (*c.*56–117), and the drama *Octavia praetexta* attributed to Seneca; *ibid*, 6–10. He explains Busenello's special interest in Tacitus: "The accessibility of Tacitus to a poet like Busenello and indeed, to his aristocratic audience in Venice is largely the consequence of the desperate political events that had shaken the foundations of Italian political life in the sixteenth century. The French invasion of Italy in 1494 and the half-century of warfare and depredations called by Guicciardini the *calamità d'Italia*, had devastating consequences for the Italian republics apart from Venice, whose salvation was attributed to her unique institutions. With them fell the philosophical justifications for republicanism." Ibid., p. 11.

[10] According to Wendy Heller, Venetians appreciated the skepticism of Tacitus's antimonarchical and pragmatic writings. She proposes "that the members of the Accademia degli Incogniti used Tacitus's history of imperial Rome in a highly specialized manner that went far beyond mere anti-Roman propaganda, expressing Venetian concerns with political pragmatism rather than moral censure, with civic virtue rather than withdrawal and solitude, and with the fulfillment of natural instincts rather than their suppression." See Wendy Heller, "Tacitus Incognito: Opera as History in 'L'Incoronazione di Poppea'," *Journal of American Musicological Society*, vol. 52, no. 1 (Spring 1999): p. 41.

but also because his virtue is continually diminished through the comments and behavior of others.

In other words, in *Poppea* there is no consistency in characterization nor there is some causal relationship between the characters' moral depictions and their final destinies. As with many real-life protagonists, they are not heroes but the victims of circumstance (or is it destiny?). It may seem that with my latter statement I somehow deny individual agency and celebrate a fatalistic sense that life is governed by forces that lie beyond human control. But this is exactly the point of contention for the *Incogniti*, and it could be so for today's listener as well: what if very little depends on individual action? What if life is only a game between the unreachable forces that control it without a particular logic of cause and effect? The *Incogniti* took this presumption as axiomatically true, and made of *Poppea* a true experiment in human behavior.

But as much as this opera seems like an open exercise in ethics, the premise of this exercise is entirely announced in the allegorical Prologue: while Virtue and Fortune fight between themselves over the supreme power over human nature, Love breaks up the fight and concludes that neither of them can measure up to Amor, the guiding force at whose command "the Earth changes." Furthermore, at the end of the second act, when Otho disguised in Drusilla's clothes wants to kill his former lover, Amor materializes on the stage and reveals himself as a *Deus ex machina* in a flash of lightning, thus saving Poppea's life.

The *Deus ex machina* is a common dramatic tool of seventeenth- and eighteenth-century opera. Resolving the dramatic conflict at any cost seemed to fit the early-modern craving for the spectacle of theatrical machines. More importantly, the unquestionable authority of divine forces was a convenient metaphor for monarchical power. John Bokina calls the *Deus ex machina* effect in Monteverdi's *L'Orfeo* (the apotheosis of Orfeo performed by Apollo) "the effect of absolutism upon the very form of opera." And in Poppea, *Love* becomes an absolute ruler who in the Prologue literally takes away the throne that Fortune and Virtue fight for.[11] At the end of the second act, it again exercises its unconditional power when saving Poppea's life. *I have saved my Poppea and now I will make her Empress*, sings Amor in the conclusion to the second act.

Love in *Poppea*, however, is not only represented by the character of Amor. It is omnipresent metaphorically throughout the opera in the lavish musical rhetoric that moves every dramatic action. The musical game of seduction is played by everyone and performed upon everyone. Nero and Otho are seduced by Poppea, Ottavia suffers for Nero, and Drusilla for Otho. Love is an ignoble game between the Seducer and the Desirer that, although performed in a beautiful language, also involves greed, ambition, and lust. In other words, beautiful and powerful music does not necessarily represent good deeds. On the contrary, the most eloquent and

---

[11]   John Bokina, "Deity, Beast and Tyrant: Images of the Prince in the Operas of Monteverdi," *International Political Science Review*, vol.12, no.1 (1991): p. 52.

seductive musical parts of *Poppea* are reserved for the moments of the deepest moral degradation.

This conflict in musical signification is represented at its best in the music of Poppea herself. She holds so much power because her musical rhetoric of seduction, quite broad in its range, simulates any affect necessary – yearning, passion, ecstasy, even feigned sincerity. In his work *L'imperatrice ambiziosa*, the *Incogniti* Federico Malipiero offers the explanation of Poppea's character that could be easily applied to her characterization in the opera:

> Poppea took control of Nero's will with absolute command, because Love, who shamelessly drives away all reputation in women, becomes, in the heart of the lover an enchantment without witchcraft that induces and forces men to abandon all reason in favor of senses. To such a state was Nero reduced that her merest hints were as absolute commands to him. She who wished, like all courtesans, to cover her lewd actions with the good name of matrimony, tried to send the emperor's will toward marriage which was responsible unless Octavia were publicly repudiated. ... Poppea, ... who knew she controlled his heart, in order to plunge him deeper into villainy ... through caresses and argument ceaselessly pushed him toward matrimony. She slandered him often. She silenced him with jests, calling him a youth of little spirit and no passion, still under the thumb of this tutors.[12]

Indeed, Poppea basically clears her path to the throne by the end of the first act. In the first cycle of persuasion, she assures Nero in her love, and in the second, she tells him to get rid of Seneca, the most serious obstacle to her final goal. In the introductory duet, Nero and Poppea are bidding farewell to each other. Poppea persuades Nero not to leave by displaying various affects: at first she sadly asks him not to go, then, when Nero mentions that he has to divorce Ottavia, she shows impatience. Only after hearing the wanted words from Nero (*Until Octavia is excluded by divorce from throne*), does she agree to sing a farewell. Finally, after going back to her original sorrowful mode, she occasionally bursts out (*You'll return?*) in order to secure her privileged position. The second cycle of persuasion comes in the end of the first act. Poppea again changes her faces with utmost swiftness. At first, she is modest and subdued while she questions Nero about his emotions. Once sure of his blind love, she changes from a celebratory and victorious mode to anger. She finally manages to accuse Seneca, the only enemy who stands between her and Nero. And love-struck Nero orders Seneca's suicide, thus fulfilling Poppea's ultimate goal.

---

[12]   Rosand, p. 50. Wendy Heller also discusses the process of linking bad empire with female sexuality in the circle of the *Incogniti*. Besides Poppea, they investigated the characters of other Roman ambitious women, such as Messalina and Agrippina. See Heller, pp. 39–96.

Venetian audiences would have known very well that, in a real sequence of historical events, Poppea's happiness was not long-lasting for she was, in the end, killed by Nero. The version of the story by the *Incogniti*, however, ends with an unforgettable love duet between Nero and the new empress. To listen to such beautiful music performed by the two most morally problematic characters in the opera probably represents the biggest challenge for audiences. Our experience of music consumption tells us to associate beauty with goodness, and *Poppea*'s conclusion could not be further from that. That is why the opera causes so much discomfort: beautiful music is put in the mouths of characters who do not deserve it. As in *Don Giovanni*, but more consciously and on a greater scale, the opera's creators sabotage the Platonic presumption that beautiful necessarily means good.

It is not only Poppea's part that creates so much dissonance between beauty and what stands behind it. The most confusing and dramatically least justified moments in the opera constantly reiterate the introductory allegory: there is nothing beyond the power of Love. And there is nothing romantic about this power. Allegorically speaking, to win over Fortune and Virtue, Love, like some kind of a Machiavellian ruler, has to triumph at any cost: the goal justifies the means. Ethically challenged because it governs everyone, the good and the bad: Love conquers all. This is exactly how Caravaggio depicts Amor: an irresistible boy with ominously dark-colored wings and a crooked smile casually steps over the symbols of lasting human endeavors (musical instruments, manuscripts, writing tools), flaunting his lethal spears. Caravaggio, like the *Incogniti*, emphasizes the deceptiveness of Love. This is precisely the role of Monteverdi's music: in *Poppea*, beautiful sounds are just appearances that serve to subdue human will. And from this stoicist point of view, all those who want to achieve self-preservation are threatened by music.[13]

This emotional distance of the *Incogniti*, however, is intensified by their extreme cynicism. Not even Seneca, the philosopher whose name is a synonym for restraint and strength, is spared from ridicule.[14] Right after Seneca's death,

---

[13]   Miller relates the Italian fashion of neostoicism to political and economical crises, explaining neostoic withdrawal from public life as a "remedy for corrupt politics." "It was the collapse of republican Italy that discredited Ciceronian political philosophy. The chaos and destruction of Italy and, later in the century, of France and the Netherlands, made the Senecan distaste for the civic life far more attractive." Miller, "Senecan Neostoicism," in Fenlon and Miller, p. 21.

[14]   Seneca's depiction is quite extraordinary. He is simultaneously a tragic and comical character. His words and music are mostly serious, although this seriousness may be at times performed as mockery (very low tessitura, clumsy ornamentations). His character gets understood in vastly different terms. Susan McClary, for example, claims that "the traditional respositories of patriarchal authority in *L'incoronazione di Poppea* – the husband, Ottone; the head of State, Nerone; the philosopher, Seneca – are all depicted as passive and impotent. Seneca habitually reverts to silly madrigalisms, which destroy the rhetorical effect of most of his statements." In: Susan McClary, "Constructions of Gender in Monteverdi's Dramatic Music," *Cambridge Opera Journal*, vol. 1, no. 3 (1989): p. 218. Ellen Rosand, on

for instance, a valet and a maidservant come upon each other, singing an erotic love duet only to be followed by the even more delightful display of (this time) homoeroticism in a duet between Nero and Lucan, "the wholesale repudiation of Stoic restraint."[15] Obviously, the *Incogniti* also mock stoic Virtue: dignity, heroism, emotional detachment, and the denial of bodily pleasures.[16] But even knowing this, we may find the opera's boldness of dramaturgical maneuvers (a display of plebeian lust and homosocial bonding after the dignified death of a great Roman philosopher) not entirely appropriate. It just does not seem believable that a criticism of stoicism would extend into such an unsubtle mockery.[17] This is why *Poppea* very often provokes mixed reactions. After the experience of the standard operatic repertoire, it is rather difficult to handle what appears as the unprecedented cynicism in the treatment of the issue of Love that this opera offers.

This sabotage of conventionality makes *Poppea* a deeply modern project. It is a product of Venetian libertinism that presumed to open ears, eyes, and mind to new and undiscovered possibilities. It is up to the artist to question the tradition and to ask uncomfortable questions about the surrounding world. And *Poppea*'s is a world whose moral premises are questioned in their bases: everyone becomes an opportunist in a disordered society; the ones who do not simply do not survive. So the modernity of the experiment of the *Incogniti* is not in the invention of Hamlet-like heroes, the Don Quixotes who are in conflict with themselves and with the entire world, the characters that governs modern drama from Shakespeare to Chekhov, or in operatic terms, from Gluck to Puccini. In *Poppea* there are no Shakespearean sufferers that Hauser calls "narcissistic"

---

the other hand, thinks the opposite, understanding Seneca as the perfect Incognito, the only noble character, whose suicide triggers general moral downfall. See Ellen Rosand, "Seneca and the Interpretation of 'L'Incoronazione di Poppea'," *Journal of American Musicological Society*, vol. 38, no.1 (Spring 1985): pp. 34–71. If it is indeed possible to perform Seneca's part in a very serious manner, it's quite unavoidable to recognize the ironic dimensions of both text and music given to the characters who surround him. All the dignity and nobility of his acceptance of death simply fade away in front of the childlike dissuasions made by his friends: *Life on earth is far too pleasant… Though at night I fall a sleeping, I will waken again in the morning… I would not die. Don't die Seneca*; all these lines seem so banal that they could be hardly taken seriously; not to mention the final chromatic ascension of the choir melody that adds up to a general impression of a parodied lamentation.

[15]   Rosand, p. 57.

[16]   Seneca is completely at odds with Love. The "revenge" that the *Incogniti* symbolically perform on him in *Poppea*, with the orgies of verbal and musical eroticism that follow his death, is not accidentally chosen: in one of his conversations with Nero (Act II, Scene 3), Seneca says that all the crimes that glorify the Empire are justified, but the crime inspired by a woman is utterly a plebeian misconduct.

[17]   Miller explains: "The hypocrisy of the historical Seneca inevitably made him vulnerable both to Tacitist and to neostoic critique. It was precisely his attachment to luxury while simultaneously declaring his opposition to it that put him in the same category with the sybaritic Nero." Fenlon and Miller, p. 47.

because of their incapability to create any bond with others. There are no tragic heroes, whose defeat in the end becomes a moral victory. We don't get to see the inner conflicts of their souls, for they do not question the moral ramifications of their doings. They have no reflection in them. *Poppea*'s modernity lies, however, in its experimental treatments of questions concerning social (and often literal) survival in a presumably civilized context.

This is not a direction that modern drama will take. The celebration of reason and order as social ideals will be rarely questioned so fundamentally. Instead, the focus will be on the problems of individuality: how an independent, conscious person manages to behave in a supposedly ordered society. This model will be abandoned only in the twentieth century, in the extremely elitist context of the artistic avant-garde, when the belief in human agency once more becomes challenged.

Here again we touch upon the question of *theatricality* that I discussed in the first chapter. In *Poppea*, the emotions are consciously overrepresented. As I concluded before, the illusion of representation is purposely accentuated along with the denial of equality between the good and the beautiful. This is a deliberate move on the side of the *Incogniti* that makes this opera experimental. They are questioning the ideological premises of their own culture, the premises of humanity and justice that are as controversial today as they were at the time of the opera's premiere. John Bokina, for example, writes:

> *Orfeo* followed the Renaissance-Petrarchan ideal of attempting to portray the inner psychological passions of the characters. But in *Poppea* inner passion is replaced by a superficial and supremely sensual desire. Consonant with the baroque enthusiasm for the sensuous poetry of Giambattista Marino, Franscesco Busenello's libretto for *Poppea* luxuriates in the sensuous description of external objects of desire.[18]

This may be true, but the question is how to distinguish musically between innerness and superficiality. *Poppea*'s musical passions seem superficial only because they are placed in such a controversial context. Let us just imagine for a moment Poppea's emotional outpouring in the context of romantic love story or Seneca's serious defiance to death in a heroic drama. Their words and music would certainly sound truer and as if coming "from their souls;" their sensuality would be understood as the metaphorical expressions of inner love. But the *Incogniti* wanted to sabotage precisely this illusion of truthfulness and emotional confession. Their message is often brutal in its honesty: words and sounds are just representations; they stand for emotions that may or may not be true; their appearance is just that and the truth may be utterly different.

---

[18] Bokina, "Deity, Beast and Tyrant: Images of the Prince in the Operas of Monteverdi," p. 59.

In any case, the *Incogniti* are not interested in truths. They are more concerned with the ways signs (true or not) shape social reality. But this is no less a political message than the kind of open "republican didacticism" that Bokina calls for. *Poppea* is not simply "divorced from practical political intent"; I contend that the intent exists but that it is complex and elitist, even in the context of the most radical libertinism. *L'incoronazione di Poppea* testifies to the origins of European modernity precisely because it produces more questions than answers about a current state of political and social affairs. It is customary to juxtapose Venetian secularism with autocratic Rome. But despite this centuries-long tension between Venetians and Romans, the *Incogniti* do not simply celebrate republicanism. Let's not forget that the opera concludes with the celebration of love of the two overly zealous monarchs whose atrocities stupefy today just as they did at the time of the opera's premiere. There is no perspective from which this concluding scene could be understood as the defeat of monarchism. Writing about similar conflicts in the German seventeenth-century *Trauerspiel*, Walter Benjamin concludes:

> The enduring fascination of the downfall of the tyrant is rooted in the conflict between the impotence and depravity of his person, on the one hand, and, on the other, the extent to which the age was convinced of the sacrosanct power of his role. It was therefore quite impossible to derive an easy moral satisfaction, in the manner of the dramas of Hans Sachs, from the tyrant's end. For if the tyrant falls, not simply in his own name, as an individual, but as a ruler and in the name of mankind and history, then this fall has the quality of a judgment, in which the subject too is implicated.[19]

The *Incogniti* obviously wanted to say something beyond a mere discussion of the advantages of a particular political constitution. Their intentions, though, become clearer when we take the music into account. In the previous chapter, I explained that the music for "Pur ti miro" coincides with the music of Ferrari's *Spiritual cantata*. Besides the fact that they were probably written by the same composer, more interesting is that they contain the same musical way of expressing love – the descending major tetrachord. Still more interesting, the descending tetrachord for the first time appears in *Poppea* in the most ecstatic moments of the duet between Nero and Lucan (*bocca, bocca ...*), right after Seneca's death. The *Incogniti* proclaim desire as a truly "democratic" force that does not choose champions. It governs everyone and, like death, it is blind to questions of honor.[20]

---

[19]   Walter Benjamin, *The Origin of German Tragic Drama*, trans. John Osborne (New York: Verso, 1973), p. 72.

[20]   Seneca, blind to love, does not escape death, its faithful counterpart.

On the Wheel of Fortune

I would like to take a look into another early-modern example that takes into account the rising modern dilemma of the ethics of escapism: the oratorio *San Giovanni Battista* (*St. John the Baptist*, 1675), written by Alessandro Stradella for the feast of St. John celebrated at the Roman church of Saint Crucifix. The libretto by Ansaldo Ansaldi (1651–1719) presents the well-known New Testament story of John the Baptist who, in trying to turn Herod from worldly pleasures, arouses the anger of his wife, which results in John's decapitation. The text is based on the New Testament gospel according to Mark (6: 17–21) and, occasionally, whole lines are quoted from the Bible. Stradella's oratorio *San Giovanni Battista*, like *L'incoronazione di Poppea*, raises ethical questions by denying the possibility of a "logical ending." Its openness is not only the issue of a tonally raised question at the very end, as has been remarked; rather the entire oratorio dramatization can be understood as "open."

The story of Salome – the daughter of Herod's defamed wife – is one of the great biblical stories that deal with the problem of excessive desire. The gospel presents Salome as a puppet controlled by her vengeful mother; nonetheless, she seduces Herod, her own stepfather, to get Saint John beheaded. A popular myth describes her punishment as equally horrendous: while crossing the frozen river of Sikoris, she falls into the water, and sharp ice cuts off her head; her sinful body vanishes in the river without a trace. The analogy of her destiny with Saint John's is unavoidable.

Conventionally, the dramatic peak in the retelling of Salome's story is depicted by her dance of the seven veils. In Stradella's oratorio, the central role of the dancing scene is shifted to the sonorous act of seduction: like Poppea with Nero, Salome achieves her goal of seducing Herod by means of musical rhetoric. The aria *These tears and sighs* (*Queste lagrime, e sospiri*) begins with the very dark, warm color of cellos and violas, with a Phrygian-tinged tonality that carries the emotional qualities of desire and yearning. The tension in the harmony is built through a combination of suspensions and passing or changing notes. These congested encounters between the contrapuntal lines create an atmosphere of "pathetic" woe and lamentation – the first of Salome's guises. Salome repeats her introductory theme twice, and in this moment it becomes clear that the descending F-minor melody represents her "tears and sighs" that are supposed to wheedle Herod into giving her what she wants. While the orchestra continues in the manner pregnant with tension and depth, Salome starts to develop her performance. When speaking directly to Herod (*which you see before you/ che tu miri*) she bears down upon her powerful seductive forces by combining sorrow with eroticism: although the instruments stay in F, her voice ascends to C and treats it as a tonic, moving all the way up to A♭ in the second octave. By reaching another register level, the voice creates a kind of "register dissonance" in relation to the accompaniment, signifying Salome's departure from the predictable musical means of pleading for mercy. She now manifests control and manipulates the listener (Herod) by displaying her abilities to fulfill desire, leaving the listener with the promise of another possible moment of passion. And although some of the ensuing affects would give the similar promises, *"che tu miri"* leaves a mark in the memory that is difficult to forget.

It seems as if after this effect Salome can play around and do whatever she wants to do (or sing whatever she wants to sing). In the next phrase, she suddenly moves to F major accompanied with continuo only. Soon it will become clear that the aria is neither in F, nor in E♭ major as Salome sometimes suggests, but according to the answers of the orchestral accompaniment – in C minor. As she continues, Salome will temporarily accept the C minor environment but shortly after will refuse again to settle there. While speaking of her desire she actually acts as an agent of desire, fugacious and seductive, hypnotizing the listener and making him crave fulfillment again. Even if she does cadence "properly" in C minor for a moment, she escapes very quickly and slides directly into B♭ minor. She reminds us that B♭ minor is only a guise too: while the instruments confirm B♭ minor, she returns to the pitch C (the second degree in B♭) and holds it just out of reach of the expected cadence. She does not accept to be governed in any moment, and even if she does sometimes seem to yield, it turns out to be the game of hide and seek that keeps listener's desire alive.

When she finally accepts B♭ minor, she starts another cycle of persuasion, as if all the rhetoric she has used was not enough. She returns to F minor, then pauses on the C-major chord that should be the dominant of F. Instead, she stops time, converts C-major into her own private tonic and indulges in self-satisfied ornamentations that show Salome's dominance, confidence, and strength. At one moment, it sounds as if she is completely involved in this preening mode, accompanied only by the basso continuo that moves to her beck and call. Salome soon realizes, however, that this is not the best manner in which to finish her pleading, and she returns to the introductory mood of humility and sorrow. The ornaments of victory transform into sorrowful sliding, though just before she concludes she executes one more sly detour into A♭ major before yielding to F minor. By using the affect of lamentation at the very end, the aria preserves the unity of mode. Herod might not even be conscious of the manipulation to which he was subjected – he might just feel the aroused desire and a need to evoke moments of fulfillment that Salome promised.

Salome's persuasion encourages Herod's worldly display of tetrarch power (*He shall feel my revenge!/ Provi pur le mie vendette*), followed by the Saint's melancholic answer to his enemies (*When will death finally, ... / Quando mai fia che morte*) and the dramatic conflict between the Saint and Salome (*You shall die!/ Morirai, Morirai!*). It is only after the execution, however, that the real, emotional conflict starts: Salome announces her victory (*Come now, crown me/ Sù , coronatemi*) while Herod, lost in his fear, is stunned by it (*Who amidst the common rejoicing ... / Chi nel comun gioire ...*). He hears the Baptist's voice and feels the punishment of the furies, finishing his final recitative with recognition of his sin and a wish for repentance.

Herod emphasizes his desperate repentance by singing so low as to reaching the tone D in the great octave. This "lowering" affect makes it seem as if the tragic story has come to an end. However, the construction of the last number that follows, the duet between Herod and Salome, unravels this impression and emphasizes the idea of indeterminacy as the powerful ending affect. At the very beginning of the duet, the extreme dramatic contrast between two main actors of the oratorio is established. This affective contrast is supported on both narrative and musical levels. The protagonists sing together almost the same lyrics, but their music juxtaposes extremely different affects. We hear a joyous, even gleeful Salome and a desperate Herod; we are to understand the contradiction of how the one's happiness is the other's devastation. The effect is even more powerful if we consider the fact that the first part of the oratorio also finishes with a duet between Herod and Salome, but with the two in concordance. The second duet stands as the antithesis to the first one, as its contrast or the opposite extreme. It shows how a harmonious world cannot exist. The composer's need to operate in the world of musical and dramatic extremes relates to what Maravall calls the phenomenon of the Baroque mercantilist spirit where "One's profit is another's loss" (Montagne) and "There is no benefit without harm to another" (de Tolosa). In other words, it's a zero-sum game.

The opposition is not set up clearly at the very beginning. The instrumental ritornello displays the main musical means of the piece: a dynamic tonality (with a modulation from D to A), Salome's joyous "song to be" in the violins, Herod's descending melody in the bass. However, the governing musical affects are not yet recognizable: the introduction offers a compact musical metaphor, the metaphor of a world that is neither good nor bad, as the circling ritornello reminds us; only when we begin to hear every part separately, when the actors start to speak (sing) do we see how a seemingly harmonious world is actually riddled with contradictory human's strivings and desires.

After the ritornello, the violin melody turns into Salome's victory song, and the introductory bass line becomes into Herod's lamentation. While Salome sings: *What rejoicing, what delight*, Herod answers back: *What anguish* (*Che gioire che contento/ Che martire*). The juxtaposition of such diverse feelings creates, in only a few measures, the strong affect of *antithesis* or an irresolvable conflict. Stradella reminds us that in a world based upon oppositions, one event, one happening can stir completely different emotions. He presents the characters of Herod and Salome as the opposite sides of one coin: their song shows how the same harmonic flow can simultaneously support such opposite affections as "rejoicing" and "anguish" through minute manipulations in melody and duration. It is as if this harmonic bass stands for the neutral scenery of two rather different events. It can be understand as what Maravall calls "mixture":

Music and the Modern Condition

Well, although the world is bad and adverse, it can also have manifestations of the good and favorable, not because at one extreme is one thing and at the other is contrary, but because very diverse effects can be abstracted from one and the same quality. There are no pessimistic aspects and the different optimistic aspects. Rather one would have to say that, by means of adequately manipulating the pessimistic aspects, favorable results can be obtained.[21]

The paradox becomes even more emphasized when we hear both actors singing together. Salome continues her jubilation while Herod repeats the descending tetrachord depicting his torments, now from G. The conflict of two opposite musical forces reflects the way Maravall defines the Baroque world where "the entire Universe is composed of contraries and is harmonized by disharmonies." From now on, even if both of them speak the same words, we know that they signify oppositely: musical semantics are here much more important than the narrative, and the musical code is the one that defines the meaning of the entire text.

Herod's unsuccessful *mimesis* further sharpens the conflict. Salome's part continues from G but when Herod tries to imitate her it sounds like failure: he meanders into B minor revealing what he really feels (*do I feel and experience within me/ provo e sento fra di me*). While Salome hurries back to D major even before the previous phrase properly ends (*a happier and more joyful day the world has never seen/ piu felice piu giocondo giorno al mondo non vedè*), Herod unwillingly repeats almost the same words (except that *felice* becomes *infelice* and *giocondo – men giocondo*), lowering the intonation down to E minor. The affect of achieving the contrasting emotions through different musical paces (joy through anticipation, lament through delay) is very persuasive: while Salome starts the phrase earlier, Herod delays, beginning each statement with a pause. After this, Salome now repeats the same words in an even more ecstatic way raising her part in A major; it seems that Herod follows her but he is actually "nowhere" ascending chromatically.

Finally, when Salome and Herod start to ask themselves about the reasons of their (un)happiness, it looks as if they are on the same ground, imitating each other in what at first sight may sound as joyful leaping, without a strong contrast in musical material. When the descending imitation penetrates the texture, it becomes obvious that those were not leaps of joy but the affects of frenzy and powerlessness. After being presented as contrasting forces, paradoxically they are now actually sung in the same manner. This equalization poses an ethical question: the situation in which both actors express their unawareness of the reasons of their actions reflects fatalism and disbelief in consequential behavior. The main protagonists act like the puppets on a stage while some strange force directs their acts. This effect is reemphasized when both of them are caught in the circle of a

[21] José Antonio Maravall, *Culture of the Baroque: Analysis of a Historical Structure*, trans. Terry Cochran (Minneapolis: University of Minnesota Press, 1986), p. 157.

descending sequence reminding the listener of the affect of repetition from the beginning of the duet. In this moment they are musically and ethically equalized as victims, but it is not yet clear what they are victims of.

In order to answer this question, it is interesting to discuss to whom the question "why" is posed. Both Herod and Salome sing *tell me why* (*dimmi perche*) as if there is someone else on or outside the scene who can help by giving the answer. Are they addressing Herodiade (Herod's wife and Salome's mother), God, one another, or maybe the audience? In any case, they are in wonder. Of course, it is possible to say that Herod is unhappy because he was unable to control his passion and thus he unwillingly killed the Baptist, but why is Salome unhappy? If she is a monstrous and deceitful character, why wouldn't she enjoy her victory without questioning? When she starts to ask for the reasons of her happiness the listeners may begin to doubt it, wondering if her triumph is triumph at all. The notion of human empowerment here bears many contradictions showing general skepticism concerning human agency. It reflects Marvell's claim that the baroque belief in uncontrolled forces, the belief in chance, fortune or coincidence, becomes the dominant worldview.[22] From this standpoint, the narrative maneuver also becomes clearer: the slight differences in Salome's and Herod's lyrics actually show how easily happiness becomes its opposite without any rational explanation. From this perspective, the opposites are not really so far away from each other, for they are the victims of the same force that defines their being; according to Maravall, they are *the victors or defeated of fortune.*

At this moment of doubt, however, the tonal flow becomes blurred. The questioning A major turns into B minor that excitingly drives the musical flow towards the final culmination. The chromatic steps in Herod's part and in the bass function as the usual affect of arousal (*pathopoeia*) that heighten the emotional effect towards the end. Instead of returning to D, the music only stays in its area for a short while. Whether the end is heard tonally as only a digression or as an actual modulation, it sounds quite unpersuasive. In the opening ritornello the modulation to A was made clear with a strong cadence, but the wavering harmony at the end of the duet somehow freezes the tonal flow. In the final measure there

---

[22] He gives a historical survey of the definition of fortune: "... for the ancients, it was decision of the gods, foreign to human beings – fate; for the Middle Ages, it was an event that providence caused to fall out of the regulated order so as to make the designs of God more inscrutable and frightful; for writers of the fifteenth century, it seemed to signify the manner in which the disorder constitutive of a world of crisis becomes manifest through its own development; at the height of the Renaissance, there was the appeal to the natural forces that fall beyond our voluntary activity, beyond our control; and in the seventeenth century, one can observe that this latter conception – which we call Machiavellian – turned into the idea of a forward movement of the things of the world, which certainly does not fit into a rational schema but which the informed human being can confront with a strategy, thereby coming to obtain favorable, statistically verifiable results... In the sense that reason already corresponds to the regular and predictable order of the natural world, fortune comes to be the contrary." Ibid., pp. 189–190.

is no leading tone to A major and the final triad is in a position with the third at the top. Whether we consider it as a weak ending on A or a halt on the fifth degree of D major, it is obvious that the music does not have a conclusive character. It should continue, whether to develop (in A major) or to conclude (in D, the tonality of the beginning). In both cases, the final sonority produces the effect of surprise, signifying an unanswered question.

It is not only the tonal flow that builds the impression of interruption: the last quarter note is on the first beat of the measure and the pause after the final tone creates an extremely powerful dramatic effect. After the final *perche* that ends the oratorio abruptly and suddenly, the audience is left in wonder. Is it possible that the oratorio will simply end like this? The silence after the final tones has much more powerful effect than any sound previously heard. It raises questions: why did the music just stop without any previous warning? Or maybe it will start again if I wait long enough? At the same time the listener is confronted with the silence of a sudden ending and with the expectation of continuation.

Recently, Dietrich Bartel created an extensive study of Baroque musical rhetoric, using the sources written by early modern German theorists who were the most effective in collecting and categorizing rhetorical figures of their time.[23] Bartel defines the affect of *interrogatio* as "a musical question rendered variously through pauses, a rise at the end of the phrase or melody, or through imperfect or Phrygian cadences."[24] Most of the theoreticians of the affects make a distinction between simple and figurative versions of the *interrogatio*. Humanist and theorist Joannes Susenbrotus (*c*.1484/1485 – 1542/1543) claims:

> The simple *interrogatio* is only used for the sake of inquiring and obtaining the response, in the spirit of its use. The figurative *interrogatio*, however, is not used for the sake of inquiring but helps to strengthen *various affections through questioning, such as affections of vehement assertion, pity, perseverance, indignation, admiration, and doubt.*"[25]

Although figurative interrogation is usually considered in the context of instrumental music, Johann Mattheson adds "consequently, an aria would ultimately end with an *interrogatio* in accordance with the text, in order to leaves the listeners in reflection ... After all, who does not recognize the necessity and charm of the question in all musical compositions?"[26] More recently, Eco has recognized that the absence of closure functioned as a powerful rhetorical affect

---

[23]   Dietrich Bartel. *Musica Poetica. Musical-Rhetorical Figures in German Baroque Music* (Lincoln and London: University of Nebraska Press, 1997).

[24]   Ibid., p. 312.

[25]   Ibid., p. 314. The italic emphasis is mine.

[26]   Ibid., p. 316.

by which the musical piece becomes "a potential mystery to be solved, a role to fulfill, a stimulus to quicken the imagination."[27]

The question is: what was the reason for the musical affect of interrogation? Why were audiences interested in this kind of musical rhetoric? It seems that the "charm of the question" appealed strongly to the seventeenth-century individual who was confronted with so many doubts in attempting to understand the world. The feeling of the subject's destabilization, and amazement with the impossibility of grasping the limits of being, created a strong disbelief in the subject's own importance. The simulation of indefiniteness in Hauser's words shows the human "wonder at the long unbroken breath which pervades the cosmos." This kind of art tries to communicate that there is an end somewhere even if we can neither perceive nor explain it. From this daze originates the desire to leave the thoughts, sights, and sounds unfinished.

An outcome like this obviously does not offer catharsis. To go back to Stradella's ending: Herod is punished all right, but what about Salome? Maybe she is punished too, because she is questioning her happiness, but the music says differently: hers is the affect of pure joy. Her joyous wondering could be easily understood as just a laugh at the catastrophe she created. For she, like Don Giovanni, manages to corrupt the world that surrounds her by using only powerful musical rhetoric. Unlike that of Mozart's protagonist, however, Salome's desire contaminates those around her, causing a breakdown of the social order. She is, like Poppea, a seductress who fearlessly achieves her goals.

The concluding effect of unresolved contrast works precisely in the opposite direction of catharsis: it tends to disturb and stir. It raises the moral dilemma mirroring a society that does not recognize the qualities of human reconciliation. The unsatisfactory catharsis in *San Giovanni Battista* anticipates strongly the worldview of *Don Giovanni*. Stradella did not, however, need to please the new

---

[27] Umberto Eco, *The Open Work*, trans. Anna Cancogni, (Cambridge, MA: Harvard University Press, 1989), p. 7. In order to observe the categories that question the boundaries of the whole – incompleteness, openness, interruption – as manifestations of the world in reconstruction, however, I need to explain how my take on these aesthetic categories differs from Eco's *opera aperta*. I am not interested here in symbolist or avant-garde breaks with traditional orders and hierarchies, which Eco discusses in great depth. Also, I do not discuss the multiplicity of meanings that every work offers in the process of interpretation or performance because almost every work can be considered "open" for interpretation. I'm discussing the qualities of openness that are intrinsic to the work and that are incorporated intentionally by the composer alone. The definition of the piece of music as the open work functions only if there is such a thing as the "closed work," and that is precisely how we continue to define the work of art: as an autonomous whole that has a logical beginning, development and ending. My focus is on works that by means of semantic dissonance or rhetorical indeterminacy deny the possibility of final catharsis. The work is, in this case, still bounded and well-defined, but fractured by the incapability or refusal to satisfactorily conclude. Eco is interested in the new hierarchies of language; I examine how and why the already existing ones arose and deteriorate.

mentality of the audience as Mozart did. Still working in a century that allows and even encourages the aesthetics of rupture and suspense – if partly for didactical purposes – Stradella, like the *Incogniti*, demonstrates what happens when the world of beautiful appearances prevails. In the century of Catholic renewal, lessons like these were expected and appreciated.[28]

Singing the World's Demons

The next time Salome takes the central place on a musical stage is in an expressionistic, deeply disturbing opera by Richard Strauss (1864–1949). As a horrendous depiction of psychological deterioration, Strauss's *Salome* (1905) presents a display of necrophilia as social commentary. Salome's perturbing character causes events that reflect irreparable cultural and civilizational decay, potentially inducing a feeling of guilt in its audience.[29] The ending of another expressionist opera also testifies to the failures of our civilization: the "improper" closure of Alban Berg's *Wozzeck* (1925) with the dissonant juxtaposition of scenes of death and childhood innocence reiterating the point that catastrophes caused by human behavior are perpetually the unavoidable perils of our civilization. This

---

[28] Miller explains how neostoic Virtue hides an inherently providential argument: "From the human point of view evil in the world was incomprehensible and fortune inconsistent. However, from God's perspective all that happened was simply the unfolding of a project of His own devising which was largely invisible to man. By providing and anchor, neostoic constancy took the uncertainty out of human existence and brought man closer to an appreciation of the providential plan. This argument made neoostoic consistency into a kind of *imitatio Dei*." Fenlon and Miller, p. 27.

[29] It is worth mentioning that Slavoj Žižek has a quite different take on Strauss's opera. He believes that Salome's insisting on kissing the head of St. John is an act of love, a sort of *Liebestod*. Žižek claims: "Salome twice insists to the end in her demand: first, she insists that the soldiers bring to her Jokanaan; then, after the dance of seven veils, she insists that the king Herod bring her on a silver platter the head of Jokanaan – when the king, believing that Jokanaan effectively is a sacred man and that it is therefore better not to touch him, offers Salome in exchange for her dance anything she wants, up to half of his kingdom and the most sacred objects in his custody, just not the head (and thus the death) of Jokanaan, she ignores this explosive outburst of higher and higher bidding and simply repeats her inexorable demand 'Bring me the head of Jokanaan.' Is there not something properly Antigonean in this request of her? Like Antigone, she insists without regard to consequences. Is therefore Salome not in a way, no less than Antigone, the embodiment of a certain ethical stance? No wonder she is so attracted to Jokanaan – it is the matter of one saint recognizing another. And how can one overlook that, at the end of Oscar Wilde's play on which Strauss' opera is based, after kissing his head, she utters a properly Christian comment on how this proves that love is stronger than death, that love can overcome death?" Slavoj Žižek, "The Politics of Redemption: Why is Wagner Worth Saving?" *Journal of Philosophy and Scripture* (Fall 2004), http://www.lacan.com/zizred.htm (accessed May 13, 2007).

turn to expressionism helps me to place and explain the work of Kurt Weill and Bertolt Brecht which I discuss below. For these composers comment on the same feeling of decadence and the failure of European society, but they react to this disappointment in civilization in profoundly different ways.

In order to explain this crucial difference between the culture of Vienna and Weimar, I would like to refer to the work of cultural theorist Helmut Lethen. In his study *Cool conduct: The culture of distance in Weimar Germany*, Lethen analyzes the changes in the mentality of the society of Weimar Republic.[30] In discussing the period between 1914 and 1945, he claims that war and industrialization transformed a German society based on guilt into one based on shame.[31] More specifically, after the atrocities of the First World War – a display of the enormous power and coldness of industrial machinery, which caused so much loss of life – and with continual modernization and industrial development, something changed in the way human behavior becomes culturally mediated in society:

> The desire to throw off the "enormous complication of the guilty personality,"[32] in which nineteenth-century psychology had entangled the image of the subject, finds expression in the writings of the new objectivity. In new objectivity's images, individuals are no more than motion-machines, feelings are mere motor reflexes, and character is a matter of what mask is put on.[33]

This difference in characterization is crucial for the expressionism of *Salome* and *Wozzeck*, on one side, and the works by Weill and Brecht, on the other. But the fact that there is a tendency to objectivize representation does not erase its painful cause: the disappointment with the current state of affairs. It is just that Weimar artists take different approaches in dealing with obviously agonizing problems. As we will see, Brecht's and Weill's opportunist characters are just the other side of

---

[30]   Helmut Lethen, *Cool Conduct: The Culture of Distance in Weimar Germany*, trans. Don Reneau (Berkley and Los Angeles: University of California Press, 2002).

[31]   Lethen clarifies: "Freud maintains that the conscience, which in a guilt culture acquires the function of an internal regulator, actually develops only in an advanced stage in the history of civilization. This insight, the late internalization of external authorities, inspired the cultural anthropology of the interwar years. Freud's idea honed the perception of ethnologists. It guided their search for examples of societies still in an earlier evolutionary stage, in which individual consciousness of guilt, a result of the tension existing between a strict superego and a subordinate ego, had not yet taken form. The American anthropologists Margaret Mead and Ruth Benedict found cultures of this type in their field research and termed them 'shame cultures'. Although research since the Second World War has made it evident that the strict polarization of guilt cultures and shame cultures cannot be maintained on empirical grounds, it remains instructive for our purposes as a historical model." Ibid., p. 14.

[32]   He here refers to Walter Benjamin's "Schicksal und Charakter," from *Zur Kritik der Gewalt und andere Aufsätze*.

[33]   Lethen, p. 12.

the coin from characters who display guilt, except that now the sense of alienation becomes externalized and examined; upon the recognition, acknowledgement, and acceptance, guilt turns into the socially negotiable form of shame; the authority of exterior judgment replaces the mechanism of individual auto-censorship.[34] This does not mean that the guilt is forgotten; on the contrary, its objectification and externalization makes it more present and more alive.

This becomes the theme of the New Objectivity (*Neue Sachlichkeit*), in which the dissonance between suppressed interiority and persistent focusing on surface phenomena is probably most vividly represented in the paintings of the "new objectivist" Otto Dix. Although never giving up the inner torment caused by the experience of the battlefield, in his work of the 1920s, he creates a series of paintings of the German city and its people: doctors, intellectuals, public figures are presented with a critical eye that borders on caricature. Lethen's description of the difference between expressionist and new objectivist portrait accurately describes Dix's surface-like representation:

> In the expressionist portrait of the individual, contours fragment, as if the body's surface were splintering under the force of energy radiating out from a central stimulus. In the new objectivity model, contours hold. Eyes peer out like spotlights from beneath a shielding brow, to interrogate space; the body (usually encased in a uniform, for quick sociological ranking) presents an occupational and class affiliation to the gaze of others, who similarly present and interrogate others' performance."[35]

The depiction of the sense of degradation of German society is more obvious in Dix's collective paintings: in the *Metropolis* (1928), for example, the big city is represented through the juxtaposition of the decadent night life of the rich and the

---

[34] Western liberal intellectual thinking today is based on self-censorship. From this perspective, the lack of guilt that Lethen writes about may be difficult to negotiate. Indeed, the danger of what could happen without self-questioning and individual responsibility is, as we know today, real. The 1930s led to two quite different (yet quite close) experiments in the denial of individual action: both national socialism and communism proved that, in the context of societies developed under the influence of Western culture, the primacy of a collective over individual identity does not function in practice. Twentieth-century artists whom I discuss were reprehended for the political dimension of their work. Their overt criticism of decadent community was overlooked, and their works were read as the monuments to decadence. The followers of National Socialism were offended by the pessimism of the avant-garde, not understanding that singing about one's own demons does not necessarily mean celebrating them. It may seem quite ironic, however, that those two ideologically opposed sides had the same dream of reestablishing a communitarian spirit.

[35] Ibid., p. 31.

poverty of the poor.[36] Compared with Ludwig Kirchner's (1880–1938) expressionist disintegration of traditional representation (the explosion of form and color in depicting the streets of Berlin in 1905) for example, Dix appears to return to more representational but almost cartoonish figure painting. This strategy performs the denial of representation, not through literal disintegration of the convention but through its ironical examination. This could also serve as a convenient description of the difference between musical expressionism of the Second Viennese school and the musical style developed in the Weimar Republic.[37] The opus of Bertolt Brecht and Kurt Weill brings about an entirely different set of questions, which nonetheless continues the questioning of the notion of the whole already begun in Viennese expressionism.

But to go back to the spirit of the time: while depicting the general zeitgeist of the period, Lethen connects seemingly unrelated Weimar cultural texts and explains their common ground. Lethen claims: "Underneath the political differences fantastic alliances developed: all of a sudden we glimpse a subterranean link between Jünger and Brecht, Benjamin and Schmitt, Krauss and Serner."[38] All these unlikely neighbors, says Lethen, venerated a conduct code borrowed from the seventeenth century. The link that Lethen finds between the different writings and avant-garde tendencies of Weimar Germany is the discovery of the phenomenon of a pre-bourgeois "rational type." He traces the keywords of Weimar

---

[36]   Janet Ward, for example, mainly defines the New Objectivity as the reflection of urban life: "New Objectivity's 'non-style,' or rejection of decorative style, constitutes this century's most concentrated systematization of surface, and has become one of European modernism's best-known visual codes. Its discursive figures include such terms as 'façade culture,' 'glamour,' 'asphalt,' and 'surface' (Fassadenkultur, Glanz, Asphalt, Oberfläche), which appeared repeatedly in the media and literature of the era to describe the modern urban, commercial experience." Janet Ward. *Weimar Surfaces: Urban Visual Culture in 1920s Germany* (Berkley: University California Press, 2001), p. 9.

[37]   The connection between music and the aesthetics of the New Objectivity may be more difficult to define. Music was not studied at the Bauhaus, and compositions performed at exhibitions of the New Objectivity were written in various styles. From today's point of view it may seem rather curious to consider Stefan Wolpe as the epitome of Weimar sensibility and, at the same time, to acknowledge that Kandinsky planned to hire Arnold Schoenberg as the director of the Weimar Music Academy. If I had to define the music of the New Objectivity, however, I would do it in very broad terms. Generally speaking, the composers of the New Objectivity used rather reduced musical means while still preserving the elements of expressionist dissonance. Compared to Stravinsky's neoclassical language or to that by *Les Six*, the music of the *New Objectivists* hides a certain kind of dissonant tension that never pervades, but always persists in the background. This could be said for Weill, but also for other composers who at some point followed the trend – for instance, Ernst Krenek (1900–1991), Paul Hindemith (1895–1963), and Stephan Wolpe (1902–1972).

[38]   Ibid., p. 12.

cool conduct – artifice, shame, outward gaze, surface psychology, functional ego, and polarization – in the culture of the Baroque.

In the century with so many conflicts and changes, everyday existence required very pragmatic instructions, and the writings of the time testify to the cultivation of survival skills. Similarly, the postwar shift in mentality in the Weimar republic that Lethen detects transforms a society of guilt into a society of shame. In the process of collective psychological self-defense, and unable to confront the atrocities of war, society replaces the notions of conscience and bourgeois "wordless interiority" with a new mentality of a functional ego that operates within the codes of cool conduct. "Man is artificial by nature," Lethen quotes the anthropologist Helmuth Plessner, the most persistent ideologist of new objectivity. The mentality shift is dialectical across many lines: it replaces the notion of culture with that of civilization, values society over community and gesture over expression. Lethen emphasizes Plessner's enchantment with a seventeenth-century notion of morality, and the delight of the avant-garde, especially the Dadaists, with the discovery of a pre-bourgeois pragmatic attitude towards the voice of conscience. Like the seventeenth-century Jesuit Balthasar Gracián, Plessner is concerned with behavior (not belief!) and its repercussions, and with the effects of social ceremony, diplomacy and tact. In the modern context, the code of cool conduct relies on the metaphor of traffic – it is shaped only by the outward signs that regulate social motion. Its motto is: "Not expression – but signals; not substance – but motion!"

The question is: would German society ever have resurrected the society of shame if not for the First World War? The Germans had to deal with defeat, and at the same time, accept the responsibility for the horror of aggression that had arisen from a presumably civilized and enlightened society. Cool conduct ends up being a vessel of defense, a therapeutic solution for a disappointed collective. And Lethen recognizes the same motive in the Jesuit code of conduct. Tormented with the long-lasting wars and crisis of faith, the Catholic communities of the seventeenth century went through very similar process of denial and rationalization as inter-war German society.

Lethen's conclusions about the twentieth-century fascination with seventeenth-century conduct of behavior conveniently support my transhistorical perspective. In his opinion, "the phenomenon of a prebourgeois 'rational type' – a person who was able to adapt personal behavior to external influences with no feelings of guilt – was the parallel discovery of a number of historical anthropologists in the 1930s."[39] In addition, he discusses the fascination of Werner Krauss (1900–1976), an expert in Romance literature, with the work by Jesuit Balthasar Gracián and his mid-seventeenth century rules of conduct, *The Art of Worldly Wisdom*. If Gracián's conduct manual could be summed up in one word that would be "self-control": it is of the utmost importance to know how to conduct oneself moderately, never revealing too much weakness. Lethen deepens the argument by commenting on the relationship between two ways of thinking:

---

[39]   Lethen, p. 5.

Suddenly visible in the distant mirror of the seventeenth century are the essential features of a heroic attitude in the twentieth: the constructions of the philosophy of history lie in ruins; in the absence of group solidarity or autonomous historical processes, artificial apparatuses in the form of parties are forming; the people are not to be trusted.[40]

This argument brings us back to the rhetorical world of *Poppea*: people are not to be trusted, and survival is possible only if the one knows how to behave; there is no guilt involved (individuals like Otho who show at least a bit of it depend on the mercy of others). The same case as with Stradella's oratorio: the characters do not express guilt; they are only stunned by the circumstances in which they find themselves. In twentieth-century works, however, responsibility and guilt cannot be ignored; they have to be dealt with. In either way it stays present: either in expressionist disintegrated subjectivity, its world and (metaphorically speaking) the work, or in a restated subjectivity that sweeps guilt under the carpet of conscience but, nonetheless, never aims at recovering its formal (and ethical) totality.

And nowhere is this twentieth-century neostoicism more obvious than in the writings of Bertolt Brecht. The key word for Brecht is "distance": the audience should be aware of what is done to them or what the goal of theater is. Unlike Aristotelian drama that enhances stage illusion and captures emotions, his epic theater should do just the opposite: deny audience-identification with the emotions of characters, and appeal not to feelings but to reason, thus raising ethical awareness. Brecht elaborates his distrust of the alleged verisimilitude of Aristotelian dramatic tradition, treating it as a mere fatalism:

Non-Aristotelian drama would at all costs avoid bundling together the events portrayed and presenting them as an inexorable fate, to which the human being is handed over helpless despite the beauty and significance of his reactions; on the contrary, it is precisely this fate that it would study closely, showing it up as of human contriving.[41]

Epic theatre, in Brecht's opinion, "arouses the spectator's capacity for action, forces him to take decisions," offers him not experience but "picture of the world" by which he is brought to "the point of recognition;" he "stands outside, studies" instead of just sharing the experience.[42] In terms of operatic genre these postulates translate into musical and dramatic procedures that are highly transparent and self-referential. First, the accent on the cooperation between the librettist and the composer refuses to blend the theatrical and the musical. The dramaturgy of the

---

[40]   Ibid., p. 41.

[41]   Bertolt Brecht, "On the Use of Music in An Epic Theatre," *Brecht on Theatre: 1933–1947: The Development of An Aesthetic*, ed. and trans. John Willet (New York: Hill and Wang, 1984), p. 87.

[42]   Brecht, "The Modern Theatre is the Epic Theatre," *Brecht on Theatre*, p. 37.

numbers is montage-like (the numbers are so strongly divided that they can stand as individual compositions), with captions displayed on the screen in between them, thereby increasing the sense of distancing through overly transparent signification of the dramatic action.

And this again brings us back to seventeenth-century musical-dramatic experiments. Brecht's postulates mirror back what was already posed as a problem by his early-modern predecessors: should musical drama deal with ethical issues through emotional catharsis or through rational observance? The answer is, of course, in the latter. Brecht shares the distaste of the *Incogniti* for the traps of stage illusions, the seduction of appearances and passive reception. He wants to empower the audience by offering a theater in which the human being is not "taken for granted," but is instead "the object of enquiry."[43] That is why he takes sides against existing forms of opera, which are merely "culinary." "It furthers pleasure even where it requires, or promotes, a certain degree of education, for the education in question is an education of taste. To every object it adopts a hedonistic approach. It 'experiences', and it ranks as an 'experience'."[44]

But let us see how these postulates of Brecht work in practice. In the *Threepenny Opera*, the street robber Macheath (Mack the Knife, *Mackie Messer*) is an anti-hero, surrounded by other anti-heroes, beggars, thieves, and whores: Peachum, the leader of the beggars who recalls morality only when Mack seduces his daughter Polly, and Jenny, a prostitute whose company puts Mack in trouble over and over again. Just before the finale, on Macheath's way to the gallows, Peachum addresses the audience in speech, breaking the illusion of dramatic realism, and announces a sudden twist: *Since this is opera, not life, you'll see justice give way before humanity. So now, to stop our story in its course, enter the royal officer on his horse* (*Damit ihr wenigstens in der Oper seht, Wie einmal Gnade vor Recht ergeht. Und darum wird, weill wir's gut mit euch meinen, Jetzt der Bote des König's erscheinen*). The resolution is forced, and its executor, the royal messenger, releases Mack and rewards him with an aristocratic title and possessions, while all the other characters comment on the event in an *all is well that ends well* manner. Throughout the opera we get to know Macheath's numerous misdeeds, but in the end he still manages to escape certain death because of this unexpected dramatic intervention – a profound parody of the operatic convention of the *deus ex machina* whereby a supposedly almighty force resolves the conflict in the plot.[45]

---

[43]   Ibid.

[44]   Ibid., p. 35.

[45]   It may seem strange that I do not take into consideration Weill's and Brecht's actual musical model for the *Threepenny Opera* – John Gay's *The Beggar's Opera* (1728), whose depiction of the street life coincided with Weill's and Brecht's interests in the social margin. John Gay's work, however, had very little impact on the development of the standard operatic European repertoire. I choose not to discuss the connections between the two

In the Brecht/Weill collaboration, as in seventeenth-century works, this dissonance in the dramatic procedure also translates into the realm of musical rhetoric: there is a tension between the music that appeals to the senses and the criticism of this very premise. As in Monteverdi's and Stradella's pieces, it is precisely this tension between cynical theater and oftentimes sensual music that makes these works so poignant.[46] The pleasure principle is simultaneously represented as both wonderful and appalling: "desire and terror continue to be both affirmative and critical; there is no clear conceptual separation between these aspects."[47]

The most obvious moment that brings together "desire and terror" is the love duet of Macheath and his former girlfriend, the prostitute Jenny. "Zuhälter-Ballade" parodies the love duet in the most profound way. Macheath and Jenny start off with a nostalgic, warm E-minor melody in tango rhythm, remembering their love story. But just after the moment when their praise to love reaches rapture in A♭ major, the melody modulates to C major. At this point, we find out rather unromantic details about their past; not exactly something to yearn for, they both nostalgically recall how Jenny's prostitution provided for both of them. The moment of operatic lyrical culmination here is laughed at with a bitter-sweet combination of taunting lyrics and care-free melody.[48]

From this perspective, the tonality and the popular character of the music can go both ways: they can cause both distancing and enjoyment. They can either be understood as signifiers of the banal and the decadent (this was probably Adorno's point of view when he favored Weill's work) or as fun and carefree (the popularity of many songs from the opera as individual pieces, like the introduction of Mac the Knife, testify to their sensual power). This beauty seems problematic because Brecht, as I explained earlier, had so much against "culinary" art – the art that seduces the senses and deactivates reasoning. And it is difficult to imagine a genre that suits this description more perfectly than opera, the genre whose history produced something as escapist as the Italian *bel canto*.

---

works at this point because that that would lead me astray from my main argument of how the standardized repertoire formed and fell into crisis.

[46]   In the words of Peter Branscombe: "*Mahagonny* is most immediately attractive where it is most culinary: Brecht's path led on to the didactic plays, Weill's to a more purely lyrical theatre." Peter Branscombe, "Brecht, Weill and Mahagonny," *The Musical Times*, vol. 102, no. 1422 (Aug, 1961): p. 486.

[47]   Hans-Thies Lehmann and Regine Rosenthal, "Newness and Pleasure: Mahagonny Songs" *TDR*, vol. 43, no. 4, *German Brecht, European Readings* (Winter, 1999): p. 24.

[48]   In his essay *Von der Einheit der Musik* (1922), Feruccio Busoni writes about the death of opera. One of the epitomes of opera's deterioration, in Busoni's opinion, is the love duet. There is no place for the love duet in opera, for eroticism is a matter of life not art; there is nothing more false and ridiculous on the operatic stage, thinks Busoni. It seems that Brecht and Weill sense the same falsity in representations of love on stage when dealing with it in the *Threepenny Opera*. For a discussion of Busoni, see Philippe-Joseph Salazar, *Idéologies de l'opéra* (Paris: Presses Universitaires de France, 1980), p. 172.

Between didactism and escapism, Weill and Brecht include two extreme ethical attitudes. Nowhere is this more pronounced than in the *Rise and Fall of the City of Mahagonny*, the opera of criminals (Leokadja Begbick, Trinity Moses, and Fatty) who found the City of Nets where everything is allowed as long as it is paid for. If the *Incogniti* targeted Love (or unconstrained human striving) as the force that rules society, for Brecht and Weill, the *spiritus movens* is no doubt Money. In Brecht's opinion, Shakespeare's great plays "were followed by three centuries in which the individual developed into a capitalist, and what killed them was not capitalism's consequences but capitalism itself."[49] The often unsubtle critique of capitalism culminates at the very end of *Mahagonny* when the main character, the lumberjack Jim, stands condemned to death for not having enough money to pay for his drinking spree. The world of Mahagonny is upside down: crimes against humanity are utterly ignored, and the only misconduct is not having enough. Everything, including human life, has a market-defined price. *Mahagonny* is a metaphor that could be easily used to depict today's *globalizing experience* of materialistic over-production, the experience that, in over-saturation, oftentimes denies its ultimate goal – the possibility of happiness.[50]

As in the *Threepenny Opera*, Mahagonny is a profoundly utopian critique born out from the belief that humanistic ideals, rather than desire for power, should govern society – a critique that somewhat blurs the fact that a collective (European) history is a history of wars, conquests, and plundering. And, as in *Threepenny Opera*, this critique uncovers *Mahagonny*'s creators as privileged individuals who acquire their right to speak, sing, and comment on the problems of material over-indulgence in a society in which, for some, there is barely enough. In other words, *Mahagonny* and the *Threepenny Opera* are written by the bourgeois for the bourgeois, and their purpose and understanding are defined by this class-bounded context.[51] As with the works of the *Incogniti*, its elitism has to be accepted as axiomatic if one wants to go beyond the questions of social power. Brecht and Weill may rely on scenes from street life, but their solution is understandable only to those who possess sufficient sophisticated intellectual backgrounds (not to mention enough free time and institutional power) to blame society for the

---

[49]   Bertolt Brecht, "Shouldn't We Abolish Aesthetics?" *Brecht on Theatre*, p. 20.

[50]   The fact that both works use so many American idioms, from the topographic to musical signifiers, should not be ignored. This is the work that presages so many of the negative repercussions of the development of liberal capitalism that is culminating today in the United States.

[51]   Darko Suvin includes the works in question in Brecht's first anarchist phase. Suvin claims: "Many critics would probably agree that Brecht's plays of the first phase do a far better job at the destruction of bourgeois values than at setting up any – even implicit – new values. They do not deal in translation but in devaluation, similar to much that was happening at the time in Central Europe, from Dadaists to, say Pirandello." Darko Suvin, "The Mirror and the Dynamo: On Brecht's Aesthetic Point of View," *TDR*, vol. 12, no.1, Bertolt Brecht. (Autumn, 1967): p. 66.

social and moral demise of the individual. And their criticism is quite desperate, denying the possibility that the situation could be somehow improved. By denying individual responsibility, they actually project a desire for a social utopia in which all people are somehow treated as equal – the project that has proven a constant failure in practice.

But to go back to the subversion of dramatic procedure that we have already seen in seventeenth-century works and in the *Threepenny Opera*: in the story of the imaginary city of worldly pleasures, Brecht and Weill once again ridicule the *Deus ex machina* principle. Between the first and second acts, a hurricane approaches Mahagonny; the hurricane destroys many cities on its way, but Mahagonny gets miraculously spared from the threatening natural disaster. As in the case of a miraculous savior in *Threepenny Opera* finale, there is no logical explanation on the writer's part for the intervention: it is not quite clear how the inhabitants of Mahagonny, like the characters of *Poppea* and the *Threepenny Opera*, actually deserve this mercy. But this salvation from tragic events in *Mahagonny* is bitter-sweet. Only in the continuation to the opera does it become clear that the avoidance of catastrophe was actually not a reward: the city dwellers sink deeper and deeper into the decadent blissfulness of earthly pleasures, not knowing how to break the vicious circle. "Remember that our life on earth is purely a cold dark place where sorrow cries all day," they ironically conclude *Mahagonny*. If *Mahagonny* brings together desire and terror, by the end of the opera desire begins to terrorize.

The solution that Brecht and Weill offer, similar to that of the *Incogniti*, is not escape from the arbitrariness of the supreme authorities (be it God, Monarch or Reason) that they criticize. They just throne another principle to rule; if not Reason, then certainly something closely related to it, its collateral phenomenon, and the other side of its Janus-like face – the Absurd. Macheath will be saved not because he is good, brave, or empowered by beautiful appearances like Salome and Poppea. He will be saved because the authors decide to do so, exercising their right to protest against a drama that unjustifiably promotes causality as the ruling force in society. In life, there are no heroes, only survivors, and opera should accurately depict that truth.

But this presumed absurdity, like every *reductio ad absurdum*, hides the opposite intentions: it mourns the loss of purposeful existence and deepens the cultural pessimism that will culminate in the theater of the absurd of the 50s and 60s.[52] In other words, the releasing of Macheath should not be perceived as ethically compromising because he and all the other anti-heroes of the *Threepenny Opera* are just the victims of their social standing. The lesson of Poppea here repeats: living in a socially disordered environment does not offer the luxury of exercising morality and fairness. That is why the saving of Mack is, after all, a

---

[52] In comparison to Brecht, Beckett's and Ionesco's plays are not overtly socially engaged. Although the theater of absurd will never replicate Brecht's social commentary, his negation of traditional dramaturgy shares the absurdist sense of being devoid of purpose.

deeply humanist gesture that assumes that all humans are equal, and the ones who err do so because they do not know better or are not offered a chance. They should not be held responsible for their actions. Mack should be saved not because he is a hero but because he is human.

The fact that there is guilt or shame indicates awareness of the effects of unconstrained desire. And I believe that "awareness" is the key word for the conclusion not only to this chapter but to the whole of my discussion. To quote once again Hauser's words concerning the birth of modern man: "one has the feeling of conscious choice rather than of necessity, of driving rather than of being driven, of the spontaneous impulse being subjected to control." Hauser here, of course, is discussing early modernity in his unprecedented study of mannerism. But what changes then from early to late modernity? What are the differences between the treatment of desire in the early and late modern pieces I have looked at?

Seventeenth- and twentieth-century attitudes echo each others' piercing skepticism, which originates from discontent with a world shattered by conflict, war, and economic crises. They both react to bankrupt hierarchies of social order. The apparent "coolness" of the twentieth century, however, reveals even more: nostalgia for the loss of the empowered autonomous subject. It mourns the ideals of the Enlightenment that got lost somewhere along the way to a society governed by economic interest, production, and over-indulgence. To go back to the question of guilt: unlike their early modern counterparts, Weill and Brecht feel responsible to comment on this loss of individualism. That is why there are characters in their works that are self-reflective. But this ability does not help them in their own soul-saving. Such persons (individual characters) exist but they are not heroic; they end up being quite arbitrarily saved or condemned to death. Almost desperate in their criticism of contemporary bourgeois society, Brecht and Weill deny any possibility of individual agency and responsibility for personal actions. The utopia of humanism reaches its peak exactly in these works that lament its impossibility. They symbolically conclude modernity with its love for the fantasy of self-representation.

How Stories End

> The time has come to recognize the whole phenomenon of music as a "oneness" and no longer to split it up according to its purpose, form, and sound-medium. It should be recognized from two premises exclusively, that of its content and that of its quality.
>
> By purpose, I mean one of the three realms of opera, Church and concert, and by form, the song, dance, fugue, or sonata; by sound-medium I mean the choice of human voices or instruments, and among these are included the orchestra, quartet, and pianoforte, or the manifold combinations of all those mentioned.

Music remains, wherever and in whatever form it appears, exclusively music and nothing else ... [53]

This is how Busoni in 1922 explains "oneness" of music. My discussion has led to conclusions similar to Busoni's: the musical rhetoric that was formed in early modernity guided music for more than three centuries, permeating all musical genres. Unlike Busoni, however, who proclaims the existing musical language as almost naturally given and unchangeable ("music remains ... music and nothing else,") I have wanted to show how this alleged naturalness came to be.

It has been quite clear from the very beginning of this study that I tend to synthesize my various understandings of how music works. And, from time to time, I have expressed awareness of the dangers of this approach. There are so many questions, for instance, that could be asked about the choices I made: why focus on certain genres and not some others, why marginalize entire bodies of works and regional cultures, why select a particular body of theoretical texts. At times it may appear that I should have touched upon other phenomena and the problems related to them. Despite my synthetic approach, however, it was never my intention to come up with an all-encompassing system that would explain exactly how modern music history works. When discussing concepts of modernity and style in my introduction, I rejected the assumption that history unfolds in a systematic fashion. On the other hand, I do not wish to claim that historical events are entirely arbitrary. I do not entirely support postmodernist dismissals of historical logic, such as Lyotard's claim that "history is a development without specifiable meaning, an accumulation of trials and errors."[54] For if there are trials and errors, they exist in relation to intentions and patterns, even if these are only perceptible in retrospect.

The principal purpose of my study was to examine certain musical works and the complex network of cultural meanings that connect them; this is the only way, in my opinion, that a vast modern repertoire can matter to audiences today. As a music historian, I understand the process of writing as the reinterpretation and revitalization of music; its purpose is not merely to restore and preserve, but also to explain music's continuing capacity to move listeners. My project aims for a sort of demystification of the "classical" repertoire: its dethroning from the untouchable status of "just music" (as Busoni wanted it to be) so that it becomes approachable to everyone. Demystification, however, does not mean simplification. The power of these works (and here I would agree with Busoni) is in their quality, or more precisely, in their continual ability to reach out to audiences.

What, then, do Busoni's proclamation of music's oneness and my observations on the musical whole have in common? They are, after all, vastly different ideas: Busoni proclaims the convention as nature, and the works I have examined bring

---

[53] Busoni, p. 1.

[54] Jean-François Lyotard, *Phenomenology*, trans. T. Brian Beakley (New York: SUNY Press, 1991), p. 38.

this supposed "naturalness" in question. But here is the link: Busoni stands on the opposite side of both expressionism and the New Objectivity; he, even when discussing opera, promotes the idea of musical purity and non-referentiality that originated in the writings of the German romanticists and – more famously – from the gap between the understanding of music of Liszt and Wagner, on one hand, and Brahms, on the other.

Busoni's proclamation of musical oneness is quite extraordinary because it involves opera, which, under any circumstances, cannot become "purified" from extra-musical meaning. He actually predicts what occurred after the norms got broken: he points to the way in which Schoenberg will go after his disappointment with expression, and he even presages the direction that post-war music (which I discussed in the first chapter) will take: by considering the "oneness" of music, he proclaims the version of musical autonomy that will be of central importance for the various twentieth-century composing techniques for which the logic depends solely on music as sound and structure. At this point, music moves away from expression and becomes predominantly an intellectual endeavor, finding its way back to the *trivium* that it abandoned several centuries ago, at the beginning of what I consider as musical modernity. This return, ironically, represents the height of the modern focus on the self. Premodern and early modern composers often thought of the mathematical understanding of music as something that reflects higher orders, the harmony of cosmos or nature;[55] in the twentieth century, however, the involvement with musical techniques reflects the capability to deal with complex musical systems that do not necessarily refer to anything outside themselves. As in Stockhausen's *Gesang Der Jünglinge*, they represent the triumph of the self that (re)creates new systems independent of outside influences of nature or culture, reaching the peak of music autonomy of which Busoni dreamt. Busoni, however, had something different in mind: he was aiming at the totality of the modern musical language, which in Adorno's opinion was false because it replicates the totality of subject (work, world) when there is none. In other words, Adorno and Schoenberg proclaimed the degraded state of music as they knew it, while Busoni called for its continuation.

Busoni's dream did not come true. After the world wars, composers alienated themselves from the middle-class audience that kept (and that often keeps today) the classical repertoire alive; they isolated themselves from listeners, with compositions that often require special knowledge and understanding, possessed only by a few. Unlike the visual arts, which managed to establish themselves very well among wider audiences (to strengthen once again Martin Jay's claims about our ocularcentrism), art music just did not find its place among wider circles of listeners. Even the canonical repertoire has had immense difficulties in maintaining

---

[55]   This is an undercurrent phenomenon in Western music. At some point, almost every composer thought in these terms, trying to find connections between artistic and natural creation. The golden section, for example, as a metaphor for perfect formal symmetry was constantly referred to, from Obrecht to Debussy.

itself on the concert stage. But the latter does not mean that the language born out of early modern rhetoric is somehow forgotten. On the contrary, it is present almost everywhere: in the majority of popular musical genres, commercial and film music, and almost every genre that is in wider use today. For as art-music composers isolated themselves, negotiations of subjectivity "transferred" to popular music, especially to the "avant-garde," "alternative," and "indie" genres that reassumed the ideals of authenticity and individualism, presenting them again as ethical issues and thus continuing the modern obsession with the self as an exquisite and unique entity.

I have managed in this study only to examine certain aspects of the relationship between music and modern culture. The entire project developed from my fascination with parallels between the formation and disintegration of modernity. Focusing intensively on the music and culture of these two historical turning points, I have offered some possible ways of revisiting the musical canon, and I opened three separate themes for further investigation: How does the notion of space in musical performance change from early to late modernity? What happens with religious identity? What is the relationship between questionable musical conclusions and modern ethics? My future goal, however, would be to broaden the discussion to the modern canonical repertoire itself – that is, to the very core of musical modernity – to seek answers to the most provocative questions raised by my study. In other words, this work represents only the opening for new investigations.

Bibliography

Abert, Hermann, *Mozart's Don Giovanni*, trans. Peter Gellhorn (London: Eulenburg Books, 1976).

Adorno, Theodor W., *Quasi una Fantasia: Essays of Modern Music*, trans. Rodney Livingston (London, New York: Verso, 1992).

Adorno, Theodor W., *Sound Figures*, trans. Rodney Livingston (Stanford, CA: Stanford University Press, 1999).

Adorno, Theodor W., *Philosophy of New Music,* trans. Robert Hullot-Kentor (Minneapolis: University of Minnesota Press, 2007).

Bardi, Pietro de, "Letter to Giovanni Battista Doni", in Leo Treitler (ed.), *Source Readings in Music History* (New York: W.W. Norton & Company, 1998).

Bartel, Dietrich, *Musica Poetica. Musical-Rhetorical Figures in German Baroque music* (Lincoln and London: University of Nebraska Press, 1997).

Benjamin, Walter, *Illuminations*, ed. Hannah Arendt, trans. Harry Zohn (New York: Schocken Books, 1968).

Benjamin, Walter, *The Origin of German Tragic Drama*, trans. John Osborne (New York: Verso, 1973).

Bernhard, Cristoph, "The Tractatus," *The Treatises of Cristoph Bernhard*, trans. Walter Hilse, Music Forum, vol. 3 (New York: Columbia University Press, 1973).

Berio, Luciano, *Laborintus II* (Milano: Universal edition, 1976).

Bianconi, Lorenzo, *Music in the Seventeenth Century*, trans. David Bryant (Cambridge: Cambridge University Press, 1982).

Bokina, John, "Resignation, Retreat, and Impotence: The Aesthetics and Politics of the Modern German Artist-Opera," *Cultural Critique*, no. 9 (Spring, 1988): pp. 157–195.

Bokina, John, "Deity, Beast and Tyrant: Images of the Prince in the Operas of Monteverdi," *International Political Science Review*, vol.12, no.1 (1991): pp. 48–66.

Bokina, John, "The Dialectic of Operatic Civilization: Mozart's Don Giovanni," in *Opera and Politics, from Monteverdi to Henze* (New Haven and London: Yale University Press, 1997).

Branscombe, Peter, "Brecht, Weill and Mahagonny," *The Musical Times*, vol. 102, no. 1422 (Aug, 1961): pp. 483–484, 486.

Brecht, Bertolt, *Brecht on Theatre: 1933–1947. The Development of An Aesthetic,* ed. and trans. John Willett (New York: Hill and Wang, 1984).

Buci-Glucksman, Christine, *Baroque Reason: The Aesthetics of Modernity,* trans. Patrick Camiller (London/Thousand Oaks/New Delhi: SAGE Publications, 1994).

Bukofzer, Manfred, *Music in the Baroque Era: From Monteverdi to Bach* (New York: W.W. Norton and Company Inc., 1947).

Busoni, Feruccio, "The Essence and Oneness of Music," in *The Essence of Music and Other Papers,* trans. Rosamond Lay (London: Rockliff, 1957).

Caccini, Giulio, "Le Nuove Musiche," in H. Wiley Hitchcock (ed.) Introduction to *Recent Researches in the Music of the Baroque Era,* vol. 9 (Madison: A-R Editons, Inc., 1970).

Calinescu, Matei, *Five Faces of Modernity: Modernism, Avant-garde, Decadence, Kitsch, Postmodernism* (Durham, NC: Duke University Press, 1987).

Carter, Tim, "A Florentine wedding of 1608," *Acta Musicologica,* vol. 55, Fasc. 1 (Jan.-Jun., 1983): p. 89–107.

Carter, Tim, *Music in Late Renaissance and Early Baroque Italy* (Portland, OR: Amadeus Press, 1992).

Carter, Tim, *Monteverdi and His Contemporaries* (Aldershot–UK, Burlington–USA: Ashgate, 2000).

Certeau, Michel de, *The Mystic Fable: The Sixteenth and Seventeenth Centuries.* vol. 1, trans. Michael B. Smith (Chicago: The University of Chicago Press, 1992).

Chua, Daniel K.L., *Absolute Music and the Construction of Meaning* (Cambridge: Cambridge University Press, 1999).

Covach, John, "The Sources of Schoenberg's 'Aesthetic Theology'," *19th-Century Music,* vol. 19, no. 3 (Spring, 1996): pp. 252–262.

Eco, Umberto. "The Poetics of the Open Work," in *The Open Work,* trans. Anna Cangogni (Cambridge, MA: Harvard University Press, 1989)

Egginton, William, *How the World Became a Stage: Presence, Theatricality, and the Question of Modernity* (Albany: State University of New York Press, 2003).

Feldman, Martha, *City Culture and the Madrigal at Venice* (Berkeley: University of California Press, 1995).

Fenlon, Ian and Peter N. Miller, *The Song of the Soul: Understanding Poppea* (London: Royal Musical Association, 1992).

Foucault, Michel, "What is an Author?" in *The Foucault Reader,* ed. Paul Rabinow (New York: Pantheon, 1984).

Foucault, Michel, *The Order of Things: An Archaeology of Human Sciences,* trans. Rupert Swyer (New York: Random House, Inc., 1994).

Frank, Manfred, *Conditio Moderna: Essays, Reden, Programm* (Leipzig: Reclam Verlag, 1993).

Gay, Peter, *Weimar Culture: The Outsider and Insider* (New York: HarperTorchbooks, 1968).

Giddens, Anthony, *The Consequences of Modernity* (Stanford: Stanford University Press, 1990).

Goehr, Lydia, *The Imaginary Museum of Musical Works: An Essay in the Philosophy of Music* (Oxford: Clarendon Press; New York: Oxford University Press, 1992).

Gracián, Balthasar, *The Art of Worldly Wisdom*, trans. Joseph Jacobs (Boston and London: Shambala, 1993).

Gurevich, Aron, *Categories of Medieval Culture*, trans. G.L. Campbell (London, Boston: Routledge & Kegan Paul, 1985).

Hadden, Jeffrey K., "Toward Desacralizing Secularization Theory," *Social Forces*, vol. 65, no.3 (Mar, 1987): pp. 587–611.

Harrison, Thomas, *1910: The Emancipation of Dissonance* (Berkeley: University of California Press, 1996).

Hauser, Arnold, *The Social History of Art*, vol. 2, trans. Stanley Godman (New York: Vintage Books, 1985).

Hauser, Arnold, *Mannerism: The Crisis of the Renaissance and the Origin of Modern Art*, trans. Eric Mosbacher in collaboration with the author (Cambridge: The Belknap Press of Harvard University Press, 1986).

Heller, Wendy, "Tacitus Incognito: Opera as History in 'L'incoronazione di Poppea'," *Journal of American Musicological Society*, vol. 52, no. 1 (Spring 1999): pp. 39–96.

Hocke, Gustav René, *Die Welt als Labyrinth: Manier und Manie in der Europäischen Kunst* (Hamburg: Rowohlt, 1957).

Idel, Moshe and Bernard McGinn (eds), *Mystical Union in Judaism, Christianity and Islam: An Ecumenical Dialogue* (New York: Continuum, 1999).

Ilic, Ljubica, "Echo and Narcissus: Labyrinths of the Self in Early Modern Music," in Jessica Goethals, Valerie McGuire and Gaoheng Zhang (eds), *Power and Image in Early Modern Europe* (Cambridge Scholars Publishing, 2008).

Jay, Martin, *Downcast Eyes: The Denigration of Vision in Twentieth-Century French Thought* (Berkeley: University of California Press, 1993).

Kircher, Athanasius, "Phonosophia Anacamptica," Liber I in *Phonurgia nova, sive Conjugium mechanico-physicum artis & natvrœ paranympha phonosophia concinnatum...*(Campidonœ: per Rudolphum Dreherr, 1673).

Kristeva, Julia, *Tales of Love*, trans. Leon S. Roudiez (New York: Columbia University Press, 1987).

Lehman, Hans-Thies and Rosenthal, Regine, "Newness and Pleasure: Mahagonny Songs," *TDR*, vol. 43, no. 4, *German Brecht, European Readings* (Winter, 1999): pp. 16–26.

Lethen, Helmut, *Cool Conduct: The Culture of Distance in Weimar Germany*, trans. Don Reneau (Berkley and Los Angeles: University of California Press, 2002).

Lyotard, François-Jean, *The Postmodern Condition* (Manchester University Press, 1984).

Lyotard, François-Jean, *Phenomenology*, trans. T. Brian Beakley (New York: SUNY Press, 1991).

McClary, Susan, "Construction of Gender in Monteverdi's Dramatic Music," *Cambridge Opera Journal*, vol. 1, no.3 (Nov., 1989): pp. 202–223.

McClary, Susan, *Feminine Endings: Music, Gender, and Sexuality* (Minneapolis: University of Minnesota Press, 1991).

McClary, Susan, *Modal Subjectivities: Self-Fashioning in the Italian Madrigal* (The University of California Press, 2004).

McClary, Susan, "Mediterranean Trade Routes and Music of the Early Seventeenth Century," *Inter-American Music Review* vol.17, no. 1–2 (Winter 2007), pp. 135–144.

MacClintock, Carol (ed.), *Readings in the History of Music in Performance* (Bloomington and London: Indiana University Press, 1979).

Maniates, Maria Rika, *Mannerism in Italian Music and Culture, 1530–1630* (Chapel Hill: The University of North Carolina Press, 1979).

Maravall, José Antonio, *Culture of the Baroque: Analysis of a Historical Structure*, trans. Terry Cochran (Minneapolis: University of Minnesota Press, 1986).

Marino, Adrian, *Moderno, modernizam, modernost* (Beograd: Narodna knjiga, 1997).

Martin, John Rupert, *Baroque* (Pelican Books, 1989).

Nagler, A.M., *Theatre Festivals of the Medici 1539–1637* (New Haven and London: Yale University Press, 1964).

Nicolson, Marjorie, *The Breaking of the Circle: Studies in the effect of the "New Science" Upon Seventeenth-Century Poetry* (New York: Columbia University Press, 1965).

Ovid, *The Metamorphoses*, trans. Michael Simpson (Amherst: University of Massachusetts Press, 2001).

Panofsky, Erwin*, Idea: A Concept in Art Theory*, trans. Joseph J.S. Peake (Columbia: University of South Carolina Press, 1968).

Panofsky, Erwin, *Perspective as Symbolic Form* (New York: Zone Books, 1991).

Panofsky, Erwin, "What is Baroque?" *Three Essays on Style*, ed. Irving Lavin (Cambridge, MA: The MIT Press, 1997).

Pirrotta, Nino, *Music and Culture in Italy from the Middle Ages to the Baroque* (Cambridge, Massachussets, and London, England: Harvard University Press, 1984).

Rabb, Theodore K., *The Struggle for Stability in Early Modern Europe* (New York: Oxford University Press, 1975).

Rifkin, Joshua and Eva Linfield, "Schütz, Heinrich," *Grove Music Online*, ed. L. Macy, http://www.grovemusic.com (accessed May, 13 2007).

Roche, Jerome, "Alessandro Grandi. A Case Study in the Choice of Texts for Motets," *Journal of the Royal Musical Association*, vol. 113, no.2 (1988): pp. 274–305.

Rosand, Ellen, "Seneca and the Interpretation of 'L'incoronazione di Poppea'," *Journal of American Musicological Society*, vol. 38, no.1 (Spring 1985): pp. 34–71.

Rosand, Ellen, *Opera in Seventeenth-Century Venice: The Creation of a Genre* (Berkeley, Los Angeles: University of California Press, 1991).

Rosen, Charles, *The Romantic Generation* (Cambridge, Massachusetts: Harvard University Press, 1995).

Salazar, Philippe-Joseph, *Idéologies de l'Opéra* (Paris: Presses Universitaires de France, 1980).

Scarpetta, Guy, *L'Artifice* (Paris: B. Grasset, 1988).

Schoenberg, Arnold, *Style and Idea*, ed. Leonard Stein, trans. Leo Black (Berkeley, Los Angeles: University of California Press, 1975).

Shaw, Jennifer, "New Performance Sources and Old Modernist Productions: 'Die Jakobsleiter' in the Age of Mechanical Reproduction," *The Journal of Musicology*, vol. 19, no. 3 (Summer, 2002): pp. 434–460.

Silbiger, Alexander (ed.), *Frescobaldi Studies* (Durham: Duke University Press, 1987).

Stephan, Rudolph, Preface to Arnold Schoenberg's *Jacob's Ladder* (Universal Edition: 1980).

Steinberg, Michael P., *Listening to Reason: Culture, Subjectivity, and Nineteenth-Century Music* (Princeton, NJ: Princeton University Press, 2004).

Sternfeld, Frederick W., "Repetition and Echo in Renaissance Poetry and Music," *English Renaissance Studies, Presented to Dame Helen Gardner in honor of her Seventeenth Birthday* (New York: Oxford University Press, 1980).

Sternfeld, Frederick W., "Orpheus, Ovid and Opera," *Journal of the Royal Musical Association*, vol.113, no.2 (1988).

Stockhausen, Karlheinz, *Elektronische Musik 1952–1960* (Kürten, Germany: Stockhausen, 1991), Compact disc.

Strunk, Oliver (ed.), *Source Readings in Music History: From Classical* Antiquity *through the Romantic Era* (New York: W.W. Norton & Company, 1950).

Suvin, Darko, "The Mirror and the Dynamo: On Brecht's Aesthetic Point of View," *TDR* (1967–1968), vol. 12, no.1, Bertolt Brecht (Autumn, 1967): pp. 56–67.

Taylor, Charles, *Sources of the Self: the Making of the Modern Identity* (Cambridge: Cambridge University Press, 1989).

Todorov, Tzvetan, *The Fantastic: A Structural Approach to a Literary Genre*, trans. Richard Howard (Ithaca, New York: Cornell University Press, 1975).

Tomlinson, Gary, *Music in Renaissance Magic: Toward a Historiography of Others* (Chicago and London: The University of Chicago Press, 1993).

Treadwell, Nina, "She descended on a cloud 'from the highest spheres:' Florentine Monody 'alla Romanina'," *Cambridge Opera Journal*, 16/1 (2004): pp. 1–22.

Treadwell, Nina, "Changing Time: Temporal Perceptions in Medician Musical Theater," presented at the 2004–2005 Clark conference core program *Structures of Feeling in Seventeenth-Century Cultural Expression* directed by Susan McClary, William Andrews Clark Memorial Library, May 20, 2005.

Tschannen, Olivier, "The Secularization Paradigm: A Systematization," *Journal of the Scientific Study of Religion*, vol. 30, no. 4 (Dec., 1991): pp. 395–415.

Villari, Rosario (ed.), *Baroque Personae*, trans. Lydia G. Cochrane (Chicago and London: The University of Chicago Press, 1995).

Vinge, Louise, *The Narcissus Theme in Western European Literature up to the Early 19th Century* (Lund: Skånska Centaltryckeriet, 1967).

Ward, Janet, *Weimar Surfaces: Urban Visual Culture in 1920s Germany* (Berkley: University California Press, 2001).

Weber, William, "The Eighteen-Century Origins of the Musical Canon," *Journal of the Royal Musical Association*, vol. 114, no.1 (1989): pp. 6–17.

Weiss, Piero and Richard Taruskin (eds), *Music in the Western World: A History in Documents* (New York: Schirmer Books, 1984).

Weitz, Morris, *The Opening Mind: A Philosophical Study of Humanistic Concepts* (Chicago and London: University of Chicago Press, 1977).

Wittkower, Rudolph, *Art and Architecture in Italy 1600–1750* (New York: Penguin Books Ltd, 1986).

Wölfflin, Heinrich, *Renaissance and Baroque*, trans. Katharine Simon (Ithaca, NY: Cornell University Press, 1966).

Žižek, Slavoj and Mladen Dolar, *Opera's Second Death* (New York–London: Routledge, 2002).

Žižek, Slavoj, "The Politics of Redemption: Why is Wagner Worth Saving?" *Journal of Philosophy and Scripture* (Fall 2004), http://www.lacan.com/zizred. htm (accessed May 13, 2007).

Index